WELCOME TO THE COMMITTEE

Welcome to the Committee

*Information and guidance for a newly-elected
member of the Committee of a Golf Club*

John V Wilson FCA
Editor - The Golf Club Secretary

BROADSIDE PUBLISHING

Part of Chapter 14 is reproduced from the HSE's booklet
Health and Safety in Golf Course Management and Maintenance
by kind permission of the Controller of Her Majesty's Stationery Office

First Edition : September 1994

Published by
Broadside Publishing
Broadside
Kent Hatch Road
Limpsfield Chart
Oxted
Surrey RH8 0SZ

Tel. 0883 730270
Fax. 0883 730570

Typeset by
Copiset, Oxted, Surrey
and printed by
Ginghams, Broadbridge Heath, Horsham, Sussex

ISBN 0 9524177 0 7

Introduction

Although this book is intended primarily to be of help to newly elected members of the Committee of a Golf Club, I hope that other Committee members and Secretaries will also find it useful.

It is designed to be a source of information, rather than a book to be read from cover to cover. A detailed Contents pages and full Index at the end of the book have been included to help you find the subject you require quickly.

If, for example, you are to serve on your Green Committee, Chapters 10 & 11 on Greenkeeping will **not** make you instant experts on course management, but should help you to understand, and respond to, most of the technical and other problems which your Head Greenkeeper is likely to encounter. You should also read Appendix 1....... Similarly, if you are on the Ladies Committee, Chapter 9 on Ladies Golf and the LGU Handicapping Scheme will be of more interest to you than the preceding Chapter on the Men's SSS and Handicapping Scheme.

Chapter 12 on Golf Clubs and VAT includes, in this first edition, an explanation of the major changes in the law this year which have produced substantial financial benefits to nearly all Members' Golf Clubs.

Inevitably, in a book like this intended for a wide audience, an element of "teach your grandmothers" is bound to occur. Most of the Chapters have been written on the assumption that the reader has little previous knowledge of the subject, so I apologise in advance if some of the contents are "old hat" to you.

I am very grateful to the many people who have helped in the preparation of this book by writing or checking some of the contents. These include the two agronomists Jim Arthur and David Stansfield for writing or checking the greenkeeping articles ; Julian Bass and Jeff McGeachie (of Travers Smith Braithwaite) for legal advice ; Elaine Mackie (Administrator of the LGU) and Alan Thirlwell (Hon. Secretary of CONGU) for checking the description of their handicapping systems ; Jon Allbutt for help on the health and safety chapter; the Secretaries of the R & A, the Home

Unions and many other golfing bodies ; and in particular Duncan Ferguson for his sensible advice and for proof-reading many of the chapters. My thanks are also due to the home team - Sue and Sarah for typing most of the manuscript, and last but not least to my wife for her patience and help during the past nine months, and for mowing the lawn and emptying my wastepaper basket at regular intervals whilst the book was being written.

A list of abbreviations used in the book is given overleaf.

Your comments on this first edition, and suggestions for matters which might be added or omitted in the future, will be warmly welcomed.

September 1994   JOHN WILSON

Contents

Abbreviations etc.

ACOP	=	Approved Code of Practice
AGCS	=	Association of Golf Club Secretaries
ATV	=	All Terrain Vehicle
BIGGA	=	British and International Golf Greenkeepers Association
BTME	=	BIGGA Turf Management Exhibition
CCTV	=	Closed Circuit Television
CONGU	–	Council of National Golf Unions
COSHH	=	Control of Substances Hazardous to Health Regulations 1988
CSS	=	Competition Scratch Score
DSS	=	Department of Social Security
EGU	=	English Golf Union
EHO	=	Environmental Health Officer
GUI	=	Golfing Union of Ireland
H&SW	=	Health and Safety at Work etc Act 1974
LGU	=	Ladies Golf Union
NGCAA	=	National Golf Clubs' Advisory Association
NIC	=	National Insurance Contributions
NRA	=	National Rivers Authority
PAYE	=	Pay As You Earn (Income tax)
PPE	=	Personal Protective Equipment
R & A	=	Royal and Ancient Golf Club of St Andrews
SERPS	=	State Earnings Related Pension Scheme
SGU	=	Scottish Golf Union
SSS	=	Standard Scratch Score
STRI	=	Sports Turf Research Institute
WGU	=	Welsh Golfing Union

References at the end of many sections or paragraphs e.g. [V1/23] are to the volume and page number of a relevant, fuller article in the newsletter *The Golf Club Secretary*, published monthly since May 1991 by Broadside Publishing and now received by over 800 Golf Clubs in the UK.

Throughout this book :

- Golf Clubs means the organisations, golf clubs are those you play with.
- Committee (except in Chapter 1) means the Club's main Committee or Board.
- Societies means visiting societies.
- Secretary refers also to the Secretary/Manager, Manager, or General Manager of a Golf Club.
- Head Greenkeeper refers also to the Course Manager.
- For "he" please read "he or she".

1
The Constitution of a Golf Club

As a new Committee member, you are strongly recommended to become familiar with your Club's constitution, especially its rules. This introductory chapter may be helpful as background information or if, during your time on the Committee, your Club's own constitution and structure is to be reviewed.

The Constitutions available

The formal constitution of a Golf Club will be one of the following:

- Incorporated as a limited company, either with share capital or limited by guarantee
- An unincorporated body.

A limited company

(a) **With share capital** This is the type most commonly used for trading entities in the UK. They can be public (with suffix plc) or private companies (with suffix Ltd.), most incorporated Golf Clubs being the latter.

In a company limited by shares, the liability of the members, i.e. its shareholders, is limited to the paid-up share capital and the amount (if any) unpaid on their shares in the company. They cannot be asked to make any further contribution beyond that amount if the company is not able to meet all its liabilities on being wound up.

(b) **Limited by guarantee** The liability of members of this type of company is limited to the amount each member has guaranteed to contribute to the company if it is wound up. This will usually be a nominal sum like £1 or £5.

All limited companies have a Memorandum and Articles of Association, covering formal matters such as its objects, its constitution, voting rights of shareholders/members, appointment of directors and other officers, general meetings, and so on. Some of the usual rules of a Golf Club (see Rules below) may be included in the Articles but are more often a separate additional document.

An unincorporated body

An unincorporated body (referred to in this paragraph as a "body") is simply an association of persons joined together by their own rules and regulations It can carry on activities and incur debts like a company or an individual. Legal action against the body will normally be addressed initially to the Captain or senior officer elected by its members to head the organisation. Trustees appointed by the members to hold the land and other assets of the body can also be sued if they fail to carry out their duties as trustees as laid down in the Trustee Act 1925, or act irresponsibly against the wishes of the members.

What Constitution should a Golf Club choose?

Most Proprietary Golf Clubs will be straightforward companies limited by shares, to give their proprietary shareholders limited liability protection and to enable them to raise the capital they require.

For **Members' Golf Clubs** the choice is not so clear cut.

The advantages of being a **limited company** (limited by shares or by guarantee) are:

- Individual officers or Committee members will not normally risk personal liability for debts arising or acts done on behalf of the Club (see Chapter 3). Instead the company itself will be liable.
- When initial or further capital is required, investors and banks prefer the limited company structure which is unambiguous and with which they are familiar. The identity of persons who should execute the mortgage will be easier to ascertain.
- An incorporated Club can sue or be sued in its own name.
- The structure inherent in a limited company can facilitate the adoption of a two-tier organisation, discussed further below.
- Suppliers prefer to deal or trade with a limited company rather than an unincorporated Club.
- Investments and other assets can be held in the Club's name, not the names of the current trustees, avoiding potential problems when a trustee dies or retires.

However there are also many advantages in having an **unincorporated** Club structure :

- The Club can have a constitution entirely as it wishes, in the form of rules and bye-laws approved by its members. Those rules can include the limitation of the amount members may have to contribute (vis-a-vis other members, as the limitation may not bind third parties) in the event of the liquidation of the Club, and the indemnity from Club funds of its officers acting responsibly. The rules can also set out clearly the voting rights of members especially on any proposed sale of the Club or any part its land, and the right to share in any surplus arising on the sale of the Club or course to a third party.

- The Club will not have to comply with the legislation applicable specifically to companies nor will its Committee members with the strict regulations which apply to directors of companies.

- It avoids any possibility (in companies limited by shares) of the course or the Club being sold "over the heads" of members, very much against their wishes.

- Long-standing shareholders can become difficult to trace. Shares can pass to families who now have no continuing interest or involvement in the Club.

- The procedures for changing the rules of a Club are usually simpler than amending a limited company's Articles of Association.

Aggrieved members cannot sue their Club if it is an unincorporated body as they are the Club and the Club is the members i.e. they would be suing themselves. There are certain circumstances, though, when a member might be able to sue a Committee member, trustee or other officer of the Club.

The taxation of Members' Clubs is not affected by their constitution (see Chapter 13).

Unincorporated Clubs, despite their somewhat difficult legal status, do seem to work well in practice. However, care is needed over the contents of their rules and in the authorisation given to their officers. A limited company structure may be preferable if the Club is a substantial one with a large number of members, or when additional finance is required to fund future developments. Clubs which are already limited companies, and are used to complying with the formalities required, will probably wish to retain that structure.

In a survey carried out by *The Golf Club Secretary* in April 1994 ("The GCS Survey") 55% of the 351 members Clubs who responded were unincorporated Clubs, 29% were companies limited by guarantee and 16% were limited companies with share capital.

The Committee of a Club contemplating a change in its constitution should always obtain professional advice before putting any proposals to members or shareholders.

Committee Structure

At a conference held in November 1993, Golf Club Secretaries were invited to discuss, in syndicates, the best organisation for a Members' Golf Club. The majority view was that a two-tier structure had many advantages over one large Committee and should comprise :

(a)   **A Board of Directors** (or Management Committee in an unincorporated Club) responsible for :

- Maintenance of the Club's ethos and traditions
- Finance (including recommending rates of subscriptions, green fees, etc)
- All staff matters
- Long term planning
- Course maintenance and design
- Clubhouse services (bar, catering, etc)
- Maintenance and security of the Club's assets
- Numbers and categories of members
- Policy on allowing societies and other visitors
- Compliance with all relevant legislation.

The main objective of the two-tier structure is to achieve continuity in all the above areas of responsibility.

The Board should be a maximum of 6 - 8 full members, with each having a specific area of responsibility e.g. finance, green, membership, etc. They should be elected to serve for a minimum of three years, and to be eligible to stand for re-election for a further period of three years. The Chairman should be elected by the Board members. The Board Member responsible for finance can be given the title Hon. Treasurer.

The Captain (and perhaps the Vice Captain) should be ex-officio members of the Board. The Board Chairman would also chair all general meetings of the Club. The Secretary should report to the Board Chairman, not the Captain.

(b)   **A Committee** responsible for :

* Election of new Men members *
* All golf matters, including Men's competitions, matches, etc *
* Men's handicaps *
* Social activities *
* The professional
* Monitoring the quality of the bar and catering services
* Student and Junior members. *

*   A separately appointed Ladies Committee would be responsible for these items for the Lady members.

This Committee would be a maximum of six elected members plus the Captain (and Vice Captain if he is not amongst those six) and possibly the Ladies Captain.   Each should again be given a specific area of responsibility. The elected members would serve for three years and not be eligible for re-election until after a gap of at least three years. The Captain would chair Committee meetings.

Honorary posts such as a President or Vice President would be on neither the Board nor the Committee.

The Secretary should be a member of both the Board and the Committee. It is essential that he should be the equivalent of a Managing Director, responsible for implementing efficiently the policies laid down by the Board and the wishes of the Committee.

Communications between the Board and the Committee can be helped by :

* A liaison meeting once or twice a year attended by all members of both bodies and
* Copies of the minutes of meetings being exchanged.

The Committee should be encouraged to put suggestions forward to the Board.

Apart from the essential need for continuity mentioned earlier, the advantages of a two-tier system (which was recommended in the R & A's publication *The Way Forward*) include :

- The Captain is not burdened with the day-to-day problems of running the Club, but can enjoy his golf and social activities and being the "front man" for the Club during his year of office.

- Service on the Committee is a useful proving ground before a member is elected to the Board.

- The Secretary does not have a new "boss" each year.

It was also agreed by the conference delegates that the number of **standing sub-committees** should be limited. If a Club decides it needs to have a formal Green Committee, the Course Manager / Head Greenkeeper must be on it and the other members of that sub-committee must never attempt to tell the latter how to do his job. Under the Men's SSS and Handicapping Scheme, a Club is required to appoint a Handicap and Competitions Committee(s).

Many delegates felt that other sub-committees should only be formed when a particular subject, e.g. the Club's policy on Societies, needs to be reviewed and discussed in depth.

Comparatively few Clubs though have yet adopted the two-tier structure - only 16% in the GCS Survey - and most still have a number of active sub-committees. Clubs with just one main Committee, as expected, tend to have more sub-committees than those with the two-tier structure. These were the figures from the GCS Survey :

Percentage of Clubs with these sub-committees	*Main Committee only* %	*Two-Tier structure* %
Green	94.6	80.4
House	92.2	71.4
Finance	83.7	58.9
Handicap & competitions	83.4	73.0
Membership	47.8	42.9
Social / Entertainment	32.2	28.6
Long-term planning	26.1	17.9

Other sub-committees reported in the GCS Survey included Health and Safety, Junior, Catering/Food/Wine, "Captains"and Rules. One had a PR sub-committee, unusual for a Members' Club.

Of the 351 Members' Clubs which completed the GCS Survey, five have no standing sub-committees, seven have only one and four have only two. The highest number of sub-committees in any Club was nine.

The Club's Rules

This is a summary of the headings normally found in the rules of a Golf Club :

1. **Name of Club**
2. **Its Objects**
3. **Officers of the Club**
   - Offices to be covered
   - How nominated and elected
   - Term of office and age limitation (if any)
   - Whether can be re-elected, and if so for how long
4. **The Members**
   - Categories of membership, and voting and other rights of each (Men & Ladies):
   - Who controls maximum number in each category
   - Election procedures
   - Resignation procedures
   - Expulsion or suspension, and right of appeal
   - Liability of members
   - Bankruptcy of member
5. **The Committee (and Management Board, if any)**
   - Those entitled to serve, and number
   - How nominated (by Committee and/or by x members) and how elected
   - Term of office, and whether able to be re-elected
   - Responsibilities and powers
   - Who chairs, and whether has casting vote
   - Frequency of meetings
6. **The Trustees**
   - Number, and how elected/appointed
   - Term of office and whether able to be re-elected
   - Responsibilities and powers

7. **General Meetings**
   - Days' notice to be given
   - Who is entitled to attend, speak and vote
   - Quorum
   - Who chairs, and whether has casting vote
   - Rights of members to call one
   - Rights of members to put forward resolutions for consideration at AGM (including one regarding a change in the Rules)
   - Whether polls or proxies allowed
   - Majorities needed to pass resolutions (see 11 below)
8. **Ladies section**
   - Officers, and election thereof
   - Committee constitution etc.
   - Rights without reference to Committee e.g. to arrange matches, competitions, etc
   - Procedures at their general meetings
9. **Guests and visitors**
   - Rights of members to introduce guests and when
   - Guests, society players and other casual visitors deemed to be temporary members
10. **Entrance fees and subscriptions**
    - When payable (and how e.g. direct debit to be compulsory ?)
    - Penalties for late payers
11. **Winding up, dissolution, or sale of all or a major part of the Club's assets**
    - Any special length of notice to call general meeting to approve
    - Majority needed to approve
    - How any eventual surplus is to be shared amongst members
12. **Alteration of Rules**
    - Majority needed at a general meeting
    - Rights of, and procedure for, a member to propose a rule change
13. **Disclaimer by Club for loss or damage to members' property**
14. **Miscellaneous**
    - Confirmation that the Club will abide by
      the Rules of Golf adopted by the R & A.
      the rules of its Home Union
      the Men's SSS and Handicapping Scheme
    - Powers of Committee to make Local Rules
    - **Appointment of Handicap & Competitions Committee(s)**
15. **Interpretation of Rules (Committee's decision final)**

16. Bye-Laws

- Whether they can be made by Committee without prior reference/subsequent approval of members
- Covering such matters as dress in the clubhouse and on the course, when ladies and juniors can play, dogs, complaints, suggestions, gratuities to staff, prompt payment of bills (no credit given), Club property not to be taken away, notices to be put up by Secretary only, competitions, if and when three and fourballs are allowed, gambling and card playing restrictions, public footpaths, licensing hours, and where practice is allowed.

2
Golf Club Finances

This Chapter is about the finances of Golf Clubs, the important difference between the apparent surplus of income over expenditure and the actual cash flow over a given period, and other financial matters affecting Golf Clubs.

Income and expenditure

You will be aware that most Golf Clubs' sources of income are :

- Subscriptions
- Entrance fees (see below)
- Green fees (including Societies)
- Profits from the bar, competitions, social activities and gaming machines
- Locker rentals and trolley storage charges
- Investment income or interest receivable.

Catering, if not franchised out, usually makes either a small profit or a small loss, after taking staff costs into account.   If it is franchised out, some Clubs subsidise the franchisee, whereas others expect a monthly contribution or profit share from the franchisee, or are happy simply to break even.   The management of the Club's bar and catering facilities is considered further in Chapter 15.

The day to day expenses of the Club are either :

(a) **capital expenditure** on "fixed assets", such as course machinery and the course itself, extensions to the clubhouse, kitchen and bar equipment, computers, the Secretary's car, etc. or

(b) **revenue expenditure** under these main headings :

- Course - all other expenditure on the course
- House - expenditure such as staff costs, building repairs, rates, etc.

- Administration - all general expenses such as the Secretary's remuneration and other admin. staff costs, the professional's retainer, postage and telephone, business rates, audit fees and so on.

- Financial - interest payable, bank charges and depreciation charges (see below).

Some Clubs do not treat entrance fees as part of their annual income, and credit them instead straight to reserves. This practice is certainly appropriate in a year when, in a change of policy, the total number of members has been increased.

Capital expenditure and depreciation

Capital expenditure is written off over a period of years by an annual depreciation charge to the income and expenditure account at a rate based on the expected life of the asset - from say three years for an office computer to fifty years for a new, substantial building. Thus course machinery with an anticipated life of five years would be depreciated annually at one fifth or 20% of the original cost. After five years the written down value of that asset would be nil in the Club's balance sheet. Any profit or loss on its sale (being the sale price less its written down value)would be credited or debited respectively to the income and expenditure account in the year of sale.

Income, expenditure and cash flow

It is important to appreciate that the surplus (or loss) shown by the income and expenditure account is unlikely to equal the increase or decrease in the Club's cash resources during that year. The reasons for this are perhaps best explained by the simple example overleaf.

Income and Expenditure Account of Marvis Bay Golf Club:

Year ended 31 December 1994

Income

Subscriptions	£200,000	
Green Fees	100,000	
Bar & catering profits	50,000	
Other income	2,000	
		352,000

Expenditure

Course	120,000	
House	100,000	
Administration	80,000	
Depreciation charges	20,000	
		320,000

Surplus of income over expenditure for the year £		32,000

During the year the Club also received £13,000 in entrance fees and spent £60,000 on an extension to the clubhouse and £25,000 on a new fairway mower. Partly because some of the expenditure on the clubhouse was not paid to the builder until the next financial year, the total owing to all creditors at the year end showed an increase of £10,000 over the previous year. Following the appointment of a new Wine Committee Chairman, the value of wine stocks had increased during the year by £2,000. The amount owing by Societies and members at the year-end remained the same as the previous year.

The **Cash Flow** of the Club for the year was therefore as follows :

Surplus per Income and Expenditure account	£32,000
Add back the depreciation charge, as this was	
simply a book entry	20,000
Add entrance fees received, added to reserves	13,000
Total of incoming funds	65,000
Deduct capital expenditure (as this was not in the income and expenditure account)	(85,000)
Decrease in working capital was therefore	(20,000)
Increase in amount owing to suppliers *	10,000
Increase in wine stocks	(2,000)
Decrease in cash resources for the year therefore	£(12,000)

* Had the Club paid them more promptly, the cash balance would have been less at the end of the year.

It will be seen that although the Club's Income and Expenditure Account showed a surplus of £32,000 in 1994, its actual **cash** resources fell by £12,000 during the year.

Your Club's annual audited accounts should include a Cash Flow statement on the above lines.

Estimating future cash flow is crucial when preparing budgets for the year or years ahead.

Managing the Club's Finances

Most Golf Clubs have an Honorary Treasurer or Chairman of Finance Committee who has the responsibility of ensuring, through the Secretary, that over a period of years the Club is following sound financial policies. This involves making certain that

- The cash resources are sufficient for present and future needs and that except in emergencies, sudden increases in subscriptions are avoided
- The Club's assets are properly maintained and safeguarded
- Any surplus cash is invested so as to yield a reasonable income combined with 100% security
- Subscriptions and entrance fees are received promptly
- Suppliers' invoices are checked by each department head and countersigned by the Secretary before being paid
- Advantage is being taken of any discounts for prompt payment offered by or negotiated with suppliers
- Management accounts comparing actual results against budget are prepared at monthly or quarterly intervals
- Records are kept and regularly reviewed of other important statistics, such as the number of visitors (analysed between Societies, members' guests and casual visitors), lunches served, members in each category, etc
- Expenditure on major projects is closely monitored and kept within the budgets set by the Committee.

Other Financial Matters within the Golf Club

Collecting subscriptions by direct debit to members' bank accounts

Once the initial extra administrative work necessary to set up the system has been completed, direct debits are an effective way of ensuring the prompt payment of subscriptions, especially if the Club's policy is to allow members to pay their annual subscriptions in half-year, quarterly or monthly instalments.

The Club can only introduce direct debits if its own bank will accept it as "an originator". Before doing this the bank will require a full indemnity (in standard form) signed by two trustees on behalf of the Club. It will also need to satisfy itself that the Club has "the integrity, the administrative and financial skills" to administer the scheme.

Payment by credit transfer

This is the similar but reverse procedure to direct debits, under which staff salaries and regular suppliers can be paid by direct credits monthly to their bank account. It has the advantages of savings in bank charges and postage, and of less cheques for the Hon. Treasurer to countersign !

Signing of cheques

Some Clubs allow cheques under a certain figure to be signed by the Secretary alone, helpful when small suppliers have to be paid promptly. If your Committee are happy to permit this, it is recommended that a No. 2 current account is opened at the Club's bank and run on the imprest system*.

*Imprest system is where an account is opened with a float of say £1,000. It is then 'topped up' periodically by paying in an amount equal to the total of the cheques drawn on that account since the last topping up or since the account was opened. Thus at any time the balance on the account plus the total of the payments made but not yet reimbursed, will always equal the float figure. The imprest system is also recommended for petty cash.

Rent reviews

If your Club leases the land on which its course and clubhouse is built, it is likely to be faced with a demand for a sharply increased rent at the next rent review date. This is because many landlords are now using professional advisers to negotiate on their behalf, whose fee is based on the percentage of the increase in the rent they achieve. The substantial profits made by certain pay and play courses are being quoted - often wrongly as far as many Members' Clubs are concerned - as an indication of how profitable a golf course can be. Increased rents achieved at nearby or comparable Clubs will also be quoted as reasons for raising your Club's rent.

It is essential, therefore, to appoint a Chartered Surveyor who specialises in this work to negotiate on your Club's behalf when the next rent review occurs.

Computer systems

A number of suitable and inexpensive software packages for use on a personal computer (PC) are now available. Some are written especially for Golf Clubs, others are designed for use by small businesses generally. The software covers :

- Handicapping and competitions recording
- Membership and subscription records and billing
- Accounting , including automatic preparation of VAT returns
- Wages and salaries
- Word processing
- Membership levy systems (using electronic tills)

Spreadsheets - a form of computerised analysis paper - are also now available for use on a PC. These are invaluable for many tasks facing the Hon. Treasurer or Secretary. For example, when preparing budgets changing one figure (say the number of members in a certain category) will automatically ripple instantly through the spreadsheet to show the full effect of making that alteration.

Most software firms will now offer, for an annual fee, help and support over the telephone when needed, and regular updates of their packages.

Funding major projects

During your time on the Committee there may be discussions about a proposed major development - perhaps building an extension to the clubhouse, creating a further 9 holes, or even buying the Club and course from its present owners.

Your own accountants/auditors should be asked to advise on the best way of raising the necessary funds to complete the project. They are likely to suggest a combination of some of the following, according to the Club's circumstances:

- Existing cash resources
- Offering life memberships to a limited number of existing members
- Levies for number of years in addition to subscriptions

- Increased subscriptions
- Increased number of members
- Allowing more visitors
- Offering loan notes (or shares) to members, with benefits in the form of reduced subscriptions or reduced green fees instead of annual interest or dividends
- Loan and overdraft facilities from the bank
- Selling unwanted assets e.g. woodlands or gravel pits.

Obviously, if the financing involves short term borrowing, it is essential to have a five or ten year cash flow budget showing how and when the loans or overdraft will be repaid, and also how the interest on the loans will be met.

Insurances

The insurances needed by a Golf Club will usually include cover for

- Loss of or damage to buildings, contents and other equipment, through fire or for any other reason
- Business interruption - loss of profits for the same reasons
- Legal liabilities - employer's, public, and product
- Directors', Committee members' and officers' liabilities (but this may be unduly expensive)
- Loss of money, including fidelity guarantee
- Personal accident and/or sickness of key employees
- Risks during construction work
- Motor insurance for the Club's vehicles.

Both the EGU and the WGU recommend a comprehensive insurance package designed specially for Golf Clubs. Another firm has been offering a very similar package for some years.*

Group schemes are also sometimes offered under which, for example, members of a Club can take out, for a discounted premium, personal insurance against loss of their clubs, liability for hitting someone with a golf ball, or losses and incapacity through themselves being injured on a golf course, etc.

* Further information from (respectively) Swire Fraser Ltd Tel. 071 481 0111 and from Linaker (Western) Ltd Tel: 0272 237777.

3

Committee Members, Trustees and Directors

The constitution of Golf Clubs was considered in Chapter 1. This Chapter explains briefly the duties, responsibilities and potential liabilities of Committee members, trustees and directors, and then suggests some Committee procedures.

The Committee Members

The powers of the Committee will be delegated by the Club and its powers should be prescribed by the Club's rules. All members of the Committee must join in the exercise of the powers, unless the rules provide to the contrary. The Committee can establish its own methods and procedures, but must not exceed the powers given to it. If tasks have been delegated by the Committee to individuals or sub-committees, the Committee should request reports from them when appropriate.

Unless the rules state otherwise, the Committee cannot function by a single member. If a Committee member has acted alone, the Committee must ratify that action at its next meeting.

The Committee should meet at least as frequently as stipulated in the rules. It must exercise its powers in the interests of the Club as a whole, not in the interests of a particular section of the Committee or of the members. To avoid bias, the rules usually limit the length of time any member can serve, or provide whether such members can be re-elected immediately after retirement by rotation or only after a gap of say not less than one year.

Individual officers or Committee members may be personally liable for debts arising from orders which they have given or acts they have done on behalf of the Club, although in practice this will not be a serious disadvantage if there are sufficient Club funds to pay the debts.

You as a Committee member should :

- Read the Club's rules and understand how the powers of the Committee are circumscribed. If the rules of the Club are unclear or deficient, seek to have them improved.

- Do not make decisions alone on behalf of the Committee unless in extreme circumstances when absolutely confident that the action will be ratified at the next Committee meeting.

- Ensure that individual Committee members or sub-committees are asked to report to the Committee as frequently as is reasonable.

- Be certain that the Committee always act in the overall interests of the Club. A conflict of interest between the Club as a whole and members of the Committee must not be allowed to arise.

- Check the Club rules to see whether Committee members are indemnified against liabilities incurred in the discharge of their duties. If there is no such indemnity try to have the rules amended to insert one.

Trustees, and the ownership of the assets of a Members' Club

Individuals must always hold property (whether land or any other type of property) on behalf of an unincorporated Club which cannot hold property in its own right. In order to facilitate dealings with Club property it is common to appoint custodians or **trustees** (who need not be Club members) to hold the property, rather than have all the Club members holding the property as joint tenants.

The manner in which a particular Club holds its property is a matter of general law and of the rules of the Club in question. If there is nothing in the rules to prevent it there can be both custodians and trustees holding different types of property within the same Club.

Trustees hold property on trust for the members of the Club. The property should be made subject to the trust by a declaration of trust, either in the document which conveys/transfers the property to the trustees or, if the trustees hold the property in a different capacity already, by a separate declaration. The declaration will commonly state that the property is held upon trust for the members of the Club according to its rules, or upon trust for the members of the Club in accordance with the directions of the Committee.

Alternatively property can be held by nominated custodians (e.g. a Bank trustee company) who hold the property on a contractual basis in accordance with the rules of the Club.

Land should be held by at least two trustees.

If you are a trustee, you should

- Ensure that the assets are held in accordance with the rules of the Club.

- Satisfy yourself that there has been a valid declaration of trust over the property and take advice to ensure that the general law of trusts has been complied with.

- Check that the Club's premises are adequately insured.

- In the case of Club premises held on lease
  (a) if the landlord will agree, have a clause inserted in the lease limiting the liability of the trustees to the Club's assets and excluding personal liability, and
  (b) ensure that the lease does not contain a covenant against assignment, so that retiring trustees can assign the lease to the fresh appointees.

Directors

A Club will only have directors if it is incorporated i.e. a company limited by guarantee or a limited company with share capital.

The Companies Act 1985 requires that every company other than a private company must have at least two directors. A private company - such as most Golf Clubs which are incorporated - need only have one, but he cannot then also be the company secretary.

The directors of a Golf Club will have all the duties and responsibilities of a director under the Companies Act 1985. They must always act within the powers given to them by the Club's memorandum and articles of association.

Their liabilities as directors will include the criminal liabilities mentioned below as well as those imposed on directors of companies by other legislation, such as wrongful or fraudulent trading, or failure to disclose an interest in a transaction.

Other Officers

These will be the Secretary and the Treasurer in most Golf Clubs.

Criminal liability

Committee members and officers have responsibilities for the Club's activities which may expose them to criminal liability. The Club's failure to comply with health and safety regulations, the Gaming Act 1968 or the Licensing Act 1964 may render them guilty of an offence. Many of the offences under these provisions are such that an officer or Committee member who was not aware of the circumstances of the offence will, nevertheless, still be guilty.

In order to minimise the risk of civil or criminal liability, you as a Committee member or officer of a Golf Club should be thoroughly acquainted with the Club's rules, should always act within your powers, be as familiar as possible with all aspects of the operations of the Club and, if in doubt, obtain independent expert advice.

Committee procedures

Annual programme

An annual programme, or timetable of items to be included on the agendas for Committee meetings, will ensure that important matters are reviewed or approved at the appropriate time of the year, and are not overlooked.

Subjects which could be included in the programme are :

(a) Those concerning the following year :
   - Approval of budgets, including those for course improvements and buildings maintenance
   - Rates of subscriptions, entrance fees and green fees
   - Policy on Societies and other visitors
   - Review of staff salaries
   - Fixture list
   - Nominations for Captain, Vice Captain and new Committee members

- Preparations for the next AGM, including the design and content of the Annual Report
- Dates and times of meetings for the whole of the following year.

(b) Other items :
- Bar and catering prices
- Winter course management programme
- Long term plans
- Insurances
- Reports by Review sub-committees (see below)

Review system

Under this, a sub-committee is created to review in depth each of the principal activities of the Club, not with the intention necessarily of changing anything but just to ensure that the Club's present procedures cannot be improved. The reviews should be carried out every three to five years, with a maximum of two per year. The sub-committees would be created at the beginning of the Club's year, at the first meeting of the new Committee. They would be required to report back, with recommendations, to the Committee within three to six months.

These periodical reviews could cover
- The course, including staff and machinery
- Societies and other visitors
- Catering and bar services
- Competitions, matches and social events, plus SSS, stroke index, and local rules.
- The Club's constitution
- All the premises
- The professional
- Conditions of employment for all staff
- Membership profile by age, type, etc., differentials in subscription rates, playing rights, etc.

One of the secondary advantages of these reviews is that "impulse" changes suggested during a year can be kept in check.

[V1/19]

Long-term planning

This can sometimes be overlooked unless a senior Committee member or a sub-committee has responsibility for it. It may take the form of a 5/10-

year plan, or an agreed strategy/policy document, or simply minutes of an annual long-term policy meeting. Long-term plans should certainly be reviewed and updated each year.

[V3/21]

Terms of reference for sub-committees

These specify the matters coming within the purview of each sub-committee. They are helpful in ensuring that subjects are not overlooked or duplicated. A typical example of where confusion might arise is bar prices - are they the responsibility of the House Committee or the Finance Committee ?

[V4/3,39,44 & 45]

Role of the Chairman

The personality and experience of the Captain/Chairman of Committee meetings will usually determine both how long each meeting lasts and the effectiveness of the Committee. He should insist, for example, that Committee papers are issued well in advance of the meeting, that reports from sub-committees always include recommendations, and that as far as possible discussions on those reports is confined to the recommendations. Some Chairman make a private note in advance of how long the discussion on each item on the agenda should be allowed to last, as a way of avoiding a Parkinson's "bicycle shed" situation arising! The order of items on the agenda can also affect the length and success of a meeting.

4
The Secretary and Other Staff

A happy and efficient staff led by the Secretary are a vital ingredient of a successful Golf Club. This Chapter covers aspects of their employment and training.

The Secretary

Perhaps the most important task any Committee may be asked to undertake is the appointment of a new Secretary, because it is he who should be the Managing Director of the Club, carrying out the policies laid down by the Committee.

He must enjoy the complete support and trust of the Committee appointing him and of succeeding Committees. It is essential therefore to take up references before confirming his appointment.

The Secretary's job is no longer an easy one. He has to establish a rapport with the members without becoming too friendly with any group or clique within the Club. He must know how to deal tactfully with Committee members and the various sections in the Club, e.g. the Men, the Ladies, the Seniors and the Juniors. He needs to be knowledgeable about current law and practice in all areas of the Club's activities.

He may have to cope with having a new "boss" each year i.e. the current Captain. Even under a two-tier Committee structure (see Chapter 1) under which he reports to the Board Chairman whose appointment is for more than one year, he will still have to work closely with, and comply with the wishes of, the current Captain. He should be an experienced golfer, enjoy the game, well aware of the Rules, the handicapping systems, the types of competitions, etc.

He also has to manage all the staff in what is often a closed community. He needs to have some knowledge about course management, so that he can be sure that the Head Greenkeeper is managing the course properly and understand any problems which the latter brings to him.

He now needs to know how to use a personal computer and to be able to prepare monthly and annual accounts, budgets, maintain the membership and handicap records, etc.

Finally, he needs to be able to contribute to Committee discussions when invited to do so, and to have the ability tactfully to steer the Committee away from subjects which, for example, have been discussed at length and agreed at previous meetings.

A sample letter of appointment and job description for a Secretary was given as a supplement to the September 1992 issue of *The Golf Club Secretary*. It includes some guidelines for the Secretary, e.g. on which competitions he may play in, his role vis-a-vis Societies, membership enquiries and vetting of prospective members, control of play on the course and similar matters.

The Secretary needs to know the action he may take on his own initiative, the action he may take and advise upon afterwards, and the action he may only take after prior consultation with the person to whom he is responsible.

His remuneration package should include medical and life assurance cover, some form of pension provision, free lunches in the clubhouse, and honorary membership of the Club during his term of office for himself, his wife and children under a certain age. It may also include a house , a "company" car and an entertainment allowance of £x per week.

The Secretary is entitled to become a member of the Association of Golf Club Secretaries after being a Secretary for six months (see page 120). It runs training courses for those wishing to become Secretaries and for newly appointed Secretaries.

Greenkeepers

The Greenkeeping staff should be encouraged to join a BIGGA (see page 121) and to participate in its activities both locally and nationally.

BIGGA issues recommendations each year on the rates of pay for all levels of greenkeeping staff. These are helpful, but actual rates of pay will depend more on the relative skills of the Club's present employees, whether they are enjoying free accommodation, on the locality of the Club, the type of course, and the competition from neighbouring Clubs.

The continuing training of greenkeepers should be actively encouraged. Advice on this is now available from the Greenkeepers Training Committee (see page 122)

Greenkeepers often seem to enjoy working in particularly scruffy clothes and to overcome this, some Clubs insist that their staff wear a standard Club uniform.

House staff

These include the Steward, the Head Chef (if not the steward's wife), all the staff in the bar and kitchen, plus the cleaners if outside cleaning contractors are not employed.

The Steward and his deputies should be encouraged to join the Golf Club Stewards Association (see page 126) and to participate in its activities.

Training opportunities for House Staff are available through that Association.

Administrative staff

The Secretary will require the help of an assistant with secretarial (typing) skills and to act as the front line defence against the inevitable and frequent interruptions from telephone calls and visitors he will otherwise suffer. Many Clubs also need to have a full or part-time bookkeeper to be responsible for carrying out all the day-to-day accounting for the Club.

Other Matters concerning all staff

Employment Law

Current employment law in the UK continues to increase in complexity, partly due to the continuing influence of EC Directives. It is always worth getting expert advice from your Club's solicitors when any problems arise.

Aspects of employment law which are likely to concern Golf Clubs include

- Issuing proper **contracts of employment** to all staff.

- The increasing rights of **part-time** and of **pregnant** employees.

- The growing cost of **statutory sick pay** and **statutory maternity pay**.

- The **Transfer of Undertakings** legislation, under which employees have the right to continue in jobs on the same terms and conditions if the ownership of the Club, or a section of it, changes. This would apply, for example, on a switch from in-house catering to a franchise operation, or vice versa.

- The risk of a clain for **unfair** or **constructive dismissal** arising if the correct disciplinary procedures are not followed.

Benefits in Kind

A Head Greenkeeper or Steward living in a house or flat belonging to the Club should be able to avoid any benefit in kind assessment on him for his rent free accommodation, provided his contract makes it clear that he is required to live in the house for the proper performance of his duties.

The Revenue appears to accept that it is customary to provide such accommodation for most Golf Club staff, but not for the Secretary who may find it hard to convince his local Inspector of Taxes that there is no benefit in kind to assess.

All employees enjoying rent-free accommodation are likely to find themselves assessed to benefits-in-kind on the value of bills such as telephone, lighting and heating paid by the Club on their behalf. Their contracts should make it clear that any income tax or NIC due on these benefits in kind assessments is their responsibility.

Round sum expense allowances to staff should always be avoided as these are subject to PAYE and NIC.

PAYE and NIC

As a new Committee member you should check that the Club is keeping within the law on PAYE and NIC matters and that it is not, for example, paying casual staff out of petty cash or failing to account properly for PAYE and NIC due on gratuities (see below). PAYE and DSS audit visits are becoming more common, and penalties may be imposed if irregularities are discovered during an Inspector's visit.

Gratuities

All gratuities are subject to PAYE.

Compulsory gratuities e.g. those added to bills to Societies, are also subject to NIC and VAT but **voluntary** gratuities such as donations to the Staff Christmas Fund by members or visitors will only attract NIC if the Club as employers decides who is to receive the gratuities and actually pays out the money. If the Club is not involved in both these procedures, no NIC liability arises.

[V3/49]

Pension and Life Assurance schemes

Full time staff should enjoy the benefits of schemes providing pension provision and life assurance cover, to which the Club contributes. If the employee is also to contribute a percentage of salary towards his pension provision, there is an NIC saving if this is done by reducing the gross salary.

A group personal pension plan has some advantages over a formal pension scheme in small organisations like Golf Clubs. Younger employees are likely to gain from contracting out of the State Earnings Related Pension Scheme (SERPS).

[V3/33, V4/6]

5
The Professional and His Shop

Nearly every Golf Club still has its own professional. This Chapter considers the terms under which he is appointed and other aspects of the service he is expected to provide to both members and visitors.

The Professional as an employee

The few Clubs who wish to run their own retail outlet using their professional's shop will usually engage the professional as an employee, to give lessons, repair clubs and play with members and, if they do not have a separate manager, to run the shop. His remuneration may take the form of a comparatively modest salary plus a proportion of his earnings from teaching, playing and repairing, and, if applicable, a profit share or bonus for managing the shop successfully. His status as an employed person for PAYE and national insurance purposes is in no doubt, and he will be entitled to all the protection afforded to employees under current employment law. He may also be entitled to share in the annual staff Christmas fund donated by members.

The Professional as a self-employed person

The more common arrangement, however, is for the professional to enter into an agreement with the Club under which he is appointed its professional as a self-employed person, on terms which will include:

- The date his appointment starts and the period of notice required from either side to terminate it.

- The basis of his fees and other earnings viz
    - the retainer to be paid monthly by the Club
    - his right to keep the net profits from the shop and all his earnings from playing, teaching and repairing
    - the percentage of any green fees he is required to collect on the Club's behalf. The advantage of giving him this task instead of

the Steward is of course that the visitors then have to visit his shop and may be persuaded to buy anything from a course planner upwards.

- The **obligations of the Club**, which will include
  - providing him with a suitable shop and workshop
  - maintaining the exterior of those premises and keeping the building itself fully insured
  - installing a security system for the premises
  - indemnifying him against any liability in connection with loss or damage to the property of members or visitors left outside or inside his shop.
  - paying the rates heating and lighting bills for the shop.
  - giving him the sole rights to sell golf equipment and to carry out the duties of a golf professional in the Club's grounds.

- The **obligations of the professional**, which will include:
  - carrying out the normal duties of a golf professional
  - the number of assistants he may or should employ
  - the hours and days during which the shop must be open
  - having to display and sell a reasonable selection of golf equipment in the shop
  - if appropriate, obtaining caddies, organising the trolley shed, and providing balls for use on the practice ground or range
  - other duties such as keeping the shop clean and tidy, supplying the interior fittings, having adequate insurance cover for contents, employer's liability, etc., paying for his own telephone and installing the equipment for his workshop. (The Club may decide to provide either or both of the latter two items).

- He will also be required not to act as a golf professional at any other Club during the term of his appointment and to display clearly his scale of charges for his services.

- The extent to which he may compete in tournaments.

- Procedure during his absence on holiday or for any other reason, including the extent to which the Club's retainer will be continued during a prolonged illness.

- Whether he is to participate in the Club's health and safety policies or to be entirely responsible for his own.

- Confirmation that he is to be self-employed, responsible for the payment of his own income tax and national insurance, pension and life assurance premiums, applying PAYE, etc. to his own staff's remuneration and doing his own accounting.

- Procedure on termination of his appointment covering disposal of his stock, vacating the premises, and whether any payment may be due to him for the goodwill which he has created for the Club by the quality of the service he has provided.

- If applicable, the terms on which he and his family are provided with living accommodation by the Club.

Other matters

Contracts

The PGA provides sample contracts between a Club and either an employed or a self-employed professional. An alternative draft of the latter contract was published as a supplement to *The Golf Club Secretary* in September 1993.

The local region of the PGA will also give advice about the level of retainer it feels is appropriate for a Club in its area.

Employed or self-employed?

The DSS has been known to try to prove that the self-employed professional is in fact an employed person. Some of the tests which it applies are :

- Must the shop be open at specific times?
- Does the Club set the profit margins?
- Does the Club order supplies for the shop and say what items should be stocked?
- Must the professional be available to give lessons for a certain minimum number of hours each week?
- Does the Club fix the cost of lessons?
- Does the Club determine the proportion of shop profits which go to the professional ?
- Is the professional paid on a regular basis?

The more these questions are answered in the affirmative, the greater the likelihood of the professional being deemed to be an employee. On the other hand if the professional sets his own profit margins, chooses his own stock, decides what he wants to charge for lessons and employs his own staff, he is likely to be treated as self-employed.

There are also instances where DSS/PAYE inspectors have tried to determine that a regular monthly retainer (varying in amount only annually after review) should be treated as a salary, subject to PAYE and national insurance contributions when paid by the Club. This attempt should be resisted if the professional is clearly otherwise a self-employed person.

Becoming a professional

Anyone wishing to become a member of the PGA has to undergo a period of training for three years, under the guidance of a qualified professional. There is a probationary period of six months before the trainee has to enter into a service agreement with his employing professional, and only after that period does he lose his amateur status. The three main subjects covered during training and in the subsequent examinations are :

- the theory and teaching of the golf swing
- club repairs, and
- commercial studies to help the professional run his shop successfully.

The PGA provides support during training, and attendance at two week-long PGA courses is mandatory during each of the first two years.

Helping your professional

You will be aware that the Club professional does now face severe competition from discount golf shops in the major cities and elsewhere. Encouraging members to support him and giving him help in the way he sets out his shop, training him to be an efficient retail manager, giving him marketing advice and supporting him in other ways, will all help him to survive and to continue to provide the service which both members and visitors appreciate.

Many Clubs, on the retirement of their professional after many years' loyal service, have then made him an honorary member.

6
Members, Societies and Other Visitors

This Chapter is about the golfers who play on your course.

Members

Categories

You will be aware already of the main categories of members found in nearly all Golf Clubs, such as Full, 5 Day, Younger, Students, Seniors, Juniors, Honorary, Overseas, and Country. A few Clubs also allow $5\,^1/2$ and 6 Day members, able to play except at certain times at the weekend.

Clubs can experience problems through having too many Senior or Junior members. Lower retirement ages means that most Clubs now have a very strong Seniors section, meeting for a 'roll-up' each week or fortnight, playing many other rounds midweek and wishing to have more and more matches versus other Clubs. These Seniors may also be fortunate enough to enjoy a concessionary rate of subscription if they are over a certain age and have been members for a qualifying number of years. Some Clubs allow a Senior member's subscription to remain fixed at the rate he paid in the year before he became entitled to the concession, but this can be costly to the Club if for inflation or any other reasons ordinary subscriptions need to be increased substantially in future years. A preferred method is one under which the Senior member receives a percentage discount, increasing year by year, on the subscription otherwise payable e.g. 3.5% at age 71, 7% at age 72, and so on.

A strong Junior section is obviously to be encouraged, but if many Juniors go through to becoming Student and then Full members, the number of vacancies for other candidates can become too limited.

Vetting procedures

The importance of having the right type of members of your Club goes without saying.

Procedures for vetting vary very much from Club to Club, according to tradition and past experience. The procedures may include combinations of any of the following :

- A candidate must supply information about himself on an **application form**, including details of his address, his occupation, his membership of other Golf Clubs, and his current handicap. Further information about his education, how long he has been playing golf, whether his wife and or children play, and if so whether they hope also to join or are already members, and so on should be given on a supporting CV form.

- Each application submitted must be supported separately by a proposer and seconder, each of whom must have been a Full member for two to three years or more. Such support must take the form of a signature on the application form, and a letter to the Captain explaining why the candidate is a suitable person to become a member.

- A candidate's application must also be supported by the signatures of x number of members in the Candidates Book.

- A candidate is required to have played a round of golf with at least one Committee member.

- Each candidate with his proposer or seconder is interviewed for about quarter of an hour by a small sub-committee, comprising say two members of the Committee, plus a Trustee or Board member as its permanent Chairman and to provide continuity.

- Each candidate with his proposer or seconder is invited to meet all members of the Committee, prior to the Committee meeting at which his name is coming forward.

- After approval of the application by the Committee, each candidate's application form is pinned on the Club's noticeboard for at least a month, to allow for the possibility that an existing member may wish to lodge an objection to the candidate becoming a member.

- After that time has elapsed without comment, the Committee formally elect the candidate either as a member immediately or by placing him on a waiting list.

Many Clubs also have the excellent rule that no member can propose more than one candidate per year. This not only ensures that one member cannot swamp the Club with his cronies, but much more importantly it provides an invaluable excuse for a member to decline an invitation to propose a candidate whom he feels is not suitable.

The Ladies Committee usually have their own vetting procedures, the total number of lady members allowed having been determined by the main Committee.

Some Clubs maintain a waiting list of prospective members who have passed the voting procedures, but others cease to accept any further membership applications until the situation eases.

Priority on election is usually given to spouses and children. One Club has an annual draw from the waiting list, making sure that certain names never seem to come out of the hat..... Selection may also be by age to improve the age profile of the membership, with perhaps an upper age limit for anyone not living locally. A more scientific approach adopted by some Clubs is to select by awarding points to candidates for age, for living locally, for a low handicap, for being a relation or well-known to many members, and so on.

The stage at which Junior members have to go through the full election procedure again varies from Club to Club. Some will dispense with it if the Committee member in charge of the Junior section confirms that the young person concerned is recommended as a member, especially if that person is a son or daughter of a member. Others require the full procedure always to be applied, when the candidate reaches the age at which he is due to become a Younger or a Full member.

Suspension or Expulsion

It is important that your Club's rules should contain the powers to suspend or expel a member, making clear both the member's rights to be accompanied at any hearing, and the subsequent appeal procedures.

Rates of Entrance Fees and Subscriptions

Your Club may be amongst those whose various rates of subscription are a percentage of the Men's Full subscription. Thus Men's 5 Day and Ladies might be 75%, Students 40% and Juniors 20% of the Full rate. Ladies are sometimes required to pay the same rate as Men even though they may have different playing rights on the course e.g. restrictions at certain times at the weekend but priority on one weekday.

Entrance fees are also often a multiple of the Full subscription, the most common being $1\,^1/2$ or 2 times. In a survey amongst subscribers to *The Golf Club Secretary* in 1992/93, only 40% of Clubs charged an entrance fee to Juniors, and even less required one from Students.

A number of alternative methods of charging entrance fees when a young person reaches the appropriate age were adopted by Clubs in the Survey. They included :

- The entrance payable is reduced
  - by $^1/_5$ or $^1/_{10}$ for each year as a Junior or Student member
  - for sons or daughters of members
- The entrance fee payable is at the rate that existed when the Junior or Student member joined the Club.
- The entrance fees may be paid over a period of years.
- The entrance fee is payable in five annual instalments from say age 23 to age 27 inclusive, during which time the member is a Younger Member. His subscription in that category plus 1/5th of the entrance fee is equal to the Full membership subscription.

Members' Guests

It is now usual for Clubs to allow members to introduce and play with guests at rates of green fees much lower than those payable by other visitors. To avoid abuse of this privilege, many Clubs place a limit on the number of guests each day which a member can introduce at the discounted rate (i.e. 1,2 or 3). Others place a restriction on the number which may be introduced per month or on the introduction of the same guest more than say six times per year.

Societies

You will know that, for most Clubs, Societies have become an important source of income, generating both substantial green fees and additional bar and catering sales.

The happy integration of Society players with the members obviously requires careful planning.

Your Committee will probably already have agreed policies on the following:

- Number of Society members allowed on each weekday - both maximum and minimum.

- The date by which final playing numbers have to be confirmed by the Society's organiser and whether any penalty is payable if actual numbers are x or more % below that confirmed number.

- Whether Societies are required to pay a deposit in advance.

- The golf formats allowed. For example, some Clubs insist on foursomes being played in the morning, others sensibly ban Texas Scrambles at any time. Other Clubs actively encourage foursomes golf by offering a discount on the normal Society day fee.

- The catering facilities to be offered. An evening meal instead of a full lunch now appears to be growing in popularity.

Other information given to each Society organiser should include such matters as the opening times of the Clubhouse (and bar), standards of dress required, whether trolleys and/or buggies are allowed, availability of caddies, services available from the professional, procedure for settlement of the account, and any handicap limits for Society members.

[V3/7]

It may be worth employing a **Starter** on Society days who can ensure that both members and visitors adhere to the laid down starting times and tees, and later act as Course Marshal monitoring the speed of play on the course.

A **questionnaire** for completion by each Society organiser at the end of the day can provide useful information on the Societies' opinions on the service and facilities offered by the Club.

[V5/25]

A **Society Log** summarising the Societies which have visited during each month will give helpful management information to the Committee, and should ensure that Societies which have behaved badly are not permitted to visit again.

[V3/15]

An alert Secretary will ensure that any worthwhile Societies are invited to book a similar date for the following year, before they leave. Clubs seeking more Societies are now advertising in the golfing magazines, often offering special rates in off-peak months. Some are also producing attractive brochures. [V4/55]

Other Visitors

Your Club will also have an agreed policy about allowing casual visitors to play on the course e.g. Must they be introduced by and play with members? Must they book in advance? Must they bring with them an introduction from their Club or handicap certificate? Must they have a Club handicap below a certain level? Are times and days on which they may play restricted? Does the Club operate starting times for most of the day? and so on.

As mentioned earlier, it is now usual for green fees to be payable to the professional to encourage visitors to go into his shop.

Offering a lower rate of green fees for evening rounds may bring in extra income but tends to attract the less skilled golfers who play slowly and cause damage to the course.

Amateur Status, and the Etiquette of Golf

The R & A recently published a helpful new book* to remind amateur golfers of the rules concerning prizes, the payments of expenses, etc. The current rules are included in the book, with over 110 decisions to clarify their interpretation.

The EGU have also recently published a booklet** on golf etiquette which explains the importance of observing this aspect of the game. It should be required reading for anyone starting to play golf.

* *Decisions on the Rules of Amateur Status is available from the R & A, price £6 in Europe, £8 in the rest of the world, with 20% discount for orders of 5 copies or more.*

** *Golf Etiquette is available from the EGU at prices from 99p each or less, depending upon the number ordered.*

7
The Rules of Golf & Local Rules

Although it is the responsibility of all golfers to know and abide by the Rules of Golf, you as a Committee member will want to have a better knowledge of the Rules than most members of your Club possess.

The Rules

The Rules of Golf are approved by the Royal and Ancient Golf Club of St Andrews ("R & A") and the United States Golf Association ("USGA").

Copies of the Rules are available free of charge from Royal Insurance, Freepost (LV 7075), PO Box 144, New Hall Lane, Liverpool, L69 4HQ.

The Rules are in three sections:

I   **Etiquette** or courtesy on the course, comprising consideration for other players, priority on the course, and care of the course.   This is essential reading for anyone taking up the game.

II **Definitions** of the terms used throughout the Rules.   These defined terms are underlined the first time they appear in any Rule.

III The **Rules** themselves (34 in all).

The Rules are complex and it would be wrong - as well as impossible - to try to summarise them in this book.   However help in the interpretation and understanding of them is available in many ways.

First there is an excellent publication *Decisions on the Rules of Golf* updated annually and published at the beginning of each year jointly by the R & A USGA.   The entire Rules are reproduced in the book, but each Rule is followed by all the decisions which have been made on the interpretation of that Rule.   Cross references throughout, a very comprehensive index, and the use of two colour printing and sensible typography combine to make the book extremely easy to use.   You are strongly recommended either to buy this book or to borrow the Secretary's copy, as you cannot fail to enjoy reading it and to learn something from it.

Did you know, for example, that you cannot remove a half-eaten pear, a banana skin, or a dead land crab lying against your ball in a bunker without incurring a penalty ? (1) Or that if your ball enters a rabbit hole out of bounds and rolls under the course so that it comes to rest under ground defined as through the green, it is deemed to be in bounds so that you may still claim penalty-free relief from "holes made by a burrowing animal" under Rule 25 - 1b? (2) Or that saying after hitting a shot "That might be lost. I'm going to reload" does not count as announcing that you are playing a provisional ball ? (3) Or that it is recommended "that rakes be placed outside bunkers, as far away as possible from the bunkers as is practical and in positions where they will be least likely to affect play" ? (4)

(1) Decisions 23/3, 23/4, 23/6   (2) Decision 25-1b/23   (3) Decision 27-2a/1   (4) Decision Misc./2.

The 1994 edition of *Decisions on the Rules of Golf* is available from the R & A, price £16 including post and packing.

The R & A have also published four videos on the Rules, details of which are given in the list of R & A publications in Appendix 2 of this book (page 136).

Three **Appendices** follow the main Rules :

Appendix I Parts A and B explain when and how Committees may make and publish **Local Rules**, with several examples of suitable wording (see also Local Rules and other matters below).

Part C is a reminder of four matters which a Committee might cover in the **Conditions of a Competition** (which they are required to make under Rule 33-1) other than the obvious items such as methods of entry, eligibility, number of rounds, settling ties, etc. The four are :

* specification of the ball - for low handicap and top class events

* time of starting - penalties for being up to five minutes late

* practice - when and where it is allowed

* advice in team competitions - confirmation that Note to Rule 8 applies under which a team may appoint one person (e.g. team captain or coach) to give advice to members of that team.

Appendix II covers the **Design of Clubs** with detailed specifications and clarification of how Rule 4-1 is to be interpreted.

Appendix III sets out the specifications for the **Ball**.

Local Rules and other matters

During your time on the Committee the question of amending your Club's Local Rules is likely to come up for discussion. Here another R & A publication - *Some Notes for the Guidance of Club Committees on the Making of Local Rules and Other Matters* - is both essential reading and helpful.

This 16 page booklet begins by explaining that Rule 33-8a of the Rules of Golf enables Club Committees to "make and publish Local Rules for abnormal conditions if they are consistent with the policy of the Governing Authority for the country concerned as set forth in Appendix 1 to these Rules".

Part I covers the **Making of Local Rules**, and contains further helpful guidance, in addition to the specimen Local Rules contained in Appendix 1 of the Rules themselves, as follows:

1. *General.* This section includes a reminder that many Clubs still have printed on their scorecards Local Rules which deal with occurrences now covered by the Rules e.g. cleaning a ball on the putting green, or lifting, cleaning and dropping an embedded ball in any closely mown area through the green. There are warnings, too, against printing extracts from or rewording the Rules of Golf in Local Rules and a reminder that a penalty under the Rules may not be waived by a Local Rule without the permission of the Governing Authority for the country concerned (the R & A in the UK). It is the responsibility of the Club's Committee to interpret its Local Rules. Understandably the Rules of Golf Committee will not do this.

2. *Local Rules for abnormal conditions,* allowed under Rule 33-8a and Appendix I, Part A. These abnormal conditions can include

- obstructions where the application of Rule 24 is impractical or inequitable such as fixed sprinkler heads, overhead wires and protective screens, etc close to the line of play
- stones in bunkers
- areas requiring preservation e.g. new ground under repair
- unusual damage to the course or accumulation of leaves
- extreme wetness, mud, poor conditions and protection of course
- local conditions which interfere with the proper playing of the game
- provisional ball for ball in water hazard.

It is emphasised that Local Rules for temporary conditions should be removed as soon as possible (and therefore not printed on the scorecard).

3. *Defining Bounds and Margins (Rule 33-2a)*. This section is a reminder to the Committee that it has to define accurately the course and out of bounds, margins of water hazards, etc and gives useful examples of important points it needs to bear in mind e.g. if a defined area within a course is declared out of bounds that "its boundaries are clearly defined by stakes or otherwise". There is also a reminder that the definition of a teeing ground "a rectangular area two clubs length in depth" must not be forgotten when placing tee markers.

4. *Drafting of Local Rules*. To assist Committees, four further draft Local Rules are given on:

- out of bounds (Rule 27-1)
- water hazards (Rule 26)
- integral part of the course (Rule 28)
- ground under repair (Rule 25-1).

Part II is on **Framing regulations governing priority on the course** and is a reminder that the Club Committee has the duty of ensuring that priority on the course, as set out in Section 1 of the Rules - Etiquette is observed.

Part III gives guidance on **framing conditions for competitions**, listing eleven matters which the Club Committee should consider.

Part IV sets out the responsibilities of the Committee, the markers and the competitors for the **issuing, marking and checking of score cards**.

Part V deals with **handicaps** and explains that these are not dealt with by the Rules of Golf but under the jurisdiction and control of the appropriate National Union. It also makes clear the responsibilities of both the player and the Committee for handicaps.

Part VI covers **course records**, and when they should be recognised.

Part VII clarifies the position regarding **submission of queries on the Rules of Golf**. Under 34-3 points of doubt or dispute may only be referred to the Rules of Golf Committee through the Secretary of the Club, Association or body responsible for the competition. Queries from individuals will not be answered by that Committee.

8
The Men's Standard Scratch Score and Handicapping Scheme

A Standard Scratch Score and Handicapping Scheme for Men has been in operation in Great Britain & Ireland since 1 March 1928. The present Scheme, introduced in 1983 and most recently revised on 1 January 1993, is based on a system used by the Australian Golf Union and takes account of all scores returned by players in medal, par and stableford competitions. It is administered by the Council of National Golf Unions (CONGU) (see page 118).

This Chapter summarises the main features of the Scheme. If you are on the Handicap & Competitions Committee of your Club, it is essential that you should be familiar with the full regulations covering the Scheme, set out in the booklet available from your Secretary, or from CONGU (price £1 inc. post & packing). The National Unions (see Chapter 16)are given a certain amount of discretion under the Scheme, so you will also need to be aware of the rulings or decisions relating to the Scheme which your own Union has given.

We are grateful to CONGU for permission to quote freely from the Scheme booklet. Phrases starting with capital letters e.g. Affiliated Club, are the terms defined (and in BLOCK CAPITALS) in the booklet.

The Scheme booklet is in three sections :

Part One	Definitions of terms used throughout
Part Two	The Golf Course and the Standard Scratch Score
Part Three	The Handicapping System.

There are also nine Appendices A - I , described at the end of this Chapter.

Part One - Definitions

These include :

<u>Area Authority</u> - any authority, such as the County Unions in England, authorised by a Union to act on the latter's behalf.

<u>Affiliated Club</u> - one which is affiliated to a Union or National Authority.

<u>Home Club</u> - the Affiliated Club of which the player is a member or, if he belongs to more than one Club, the one which he has elected to be his Home Club.

<u>Member</u> - an amateur golfer eligible to compete in Qualifying Competitions (see below) arranged by an Affiliated Club, subject only to exclusion by certain restrictions e.g. handicap, age, etc.

<u>Handicapping Authority</u> - for a player it is his Home Club subject to the overall jurisdiction of the Union.   Within a Club, the Scheme must be administered by a Handicap Committee.

There are two *types* of handicap :

- <u>Exact Handicap</u> - as calculated under the Scheme, to one place of decimals
- <u>Playing Handicap</u> - Exact Handicap rounded up or down to nearest whole number (0.5 is rounded upwards)

and four *categories* :

Category 1	Handicaps of 5 or less
Category 2	Handicaps 6 - 12
Category 3	Handicaps 13 - 20
Category 4	Handicaps 21 - 28 (maximum).

The procedures for allotting and amending handicaps is described later in this Chapter.

Play should always be from the <u>Medal Tees</u>, a rectangular area the front of which must be not more than 10 yards (9 metres) in front of the Distance Point (the marker indicating the point on the tee from which the length of the hole has been measured). The rear of the Medal Tee must be not less than 2 yards (2 metres) behind the Distance Point.

A <u>Qualifying Competition</u> is one in which Medal Play Conditions prevail i.e. stroke, par or stableford competitions played with the full handicap allowance under the Rules of Golf, played from the Medal Tees, and over a course whose length varies by not more than 100 yards (91 metres) from the length of the Measured Course. The <u>Competition Scratch Score</u> (CSS) has to be calculated at the end of each Qualifying Competition, as explained below.

Part Two - The Golf Course and the Standard Scratch Score

Standard Scratch Score ("SSS") means the score expected to be returned by a scratch player in ideal weather conditions.

The SSS is determined by officials of the Union. It is based initially on the Table of Provisional Standard Scratch Scores given on page 9 of the Scheme booklet. This gives a provisional SSS according to the total length of the measured course e.g. from 7001 - 7200 yards = SSS of 74, down to 4001 - 4200 = SSS of 60. A course of less than 3000 yards cannot have an SSS. Those between 3001 and 4000 may be allocated an SSS at the Union's discretion.

The officials then take into account other factors such as :

• the terrain and layout
• the average amount of run
• size of greens and whether "holding" or not
• whether greens are well guarded
• width of fairways, nature of trees, type of rough
• location of course, and impact of usual weather conditions
• whether length of course is close to either the upper or lower limit of its band in the Table,

and adjust the provisional SSS up or down as appropriate.

From 1 January 1993, a Union can direct that the SSS shall be determined in accordance with the Scratch Score Rating Procedure of the USGA. This more sophisticated method has much to commend it and the GUI, SGU and WGU (but not the EGU) have since recommended its adoption.

The regulations of the Scheme also cover how courses are to be measured, the procedure to be followed when a course is altered, preferred lies, permitted adjustments, and the layout of tees.

The R & A recommend that Medal tee markers should be in these colours:

Men's Back	White
Men's Forward	Yellow
Ladies Standard (LGU)	Red

and that back tees for National Championships should be blue.

A Par score for each hole can be determined by the Club, and need not in total equal the SSS. The SSS must always be printed on the men's scorecard.   The Par for each hole should take into account its difficulty as well as its length, but must be within these limits :

Par 3	Up to 250 yards
Par 4	220 - 500 yards
Par 5	440 yards or more.

The Club may also determine the <u>Stroke Index</u> for each hole.

Part Three : Handicapping

The allocation of handicaps to each Member is the responsibility of a Handicap Committee which each Affiliated Club must appoint. As stated earlier, the overall jurisdiction for the administration of the Scheme lies with the Unions, who in turn may delegate certain responsibilities to the Area Authorities.

The rights and obligations of the Unions, the Area Authorities and the Affiliated Clubs are set out in the Scheme booklet (Clauses 9-11, pages 13-14).

The <u>Handicap Committee</u> has a number of responsibilities (Clause 12), which it will often delegate to the Secretary. These include:

- maintaining a list of the competitors in a Qualifying Competition
- trying to ensure that all cards taken out in a Qualifying Competition are returned
- posting immediately on the notice board all changes of members' handicaps
- ensuring that a record of all members' handicaps is displayed prominently in the clubhouse
- maintaining the records of all Qualifying Competitions and the handicap history for each member.

The player is allowed one handicap only, allotted and adjusted by his Home Club. If he is a member of more than one Club, he must elect which shall be his Home Club, and always give advance notice if he intends to change that election. He must also give his Home Club details of the other Affiliated Clubs of which he is a member. He must advise those other Clubs the name of his Home Club and whenever his handicap is altered by his Home Club. He is also responsible for reporting "away" scores in Qualifying Competitions to his Home Club (and scores in a non-qualifying competition if so directed by his Union).

The provisions regarding Qualifying Scores are set out in Clause 14 (page 16). These explain inter alia the procedures to be followed on abandoned rounds of Qualifying Competitions, and on scores on a course of reduced length. Returns which are not accepted as Qualifying Scores are :

- scores returned in a better ball fourball competition (aggregate four ball competitions are accepted)
- scores returned over less than 18 holes
- scores returned in competitions not within the Rules of Golf and Local Rules e.g. one in which the number of clubs is limited.
- scores in an extended competition where the competitor has the option of selecting the day or days on which he shall compete (with some exceptions)
- stableford and par competitions played with less than the full handicap allowance
- scores in an event run by an organisation which is not a Handicapping Authority unless the event has been previously approved by the Union as a Qualifying Competition.

Allotment of Handicaps

A handicap can only be given to a Member of an Affiliated Club.

To obtain a handicap, a Member must submit three cards, preferably over a Measured Course. Scores of more than 2 over par at any hole are amended by the Handicap Committee to 2 over. The Exact Handicap (which in this case is also the Playing Handicap) is the difference between the best adjusted score - *not* the average of the three scores - and the SSS. However the Handicap Committee is given discretion to allot a lower (or exceptionally, a higher) handicap if it judges the handicap based on the best score does not reflect the Member's playing ability.

Similarly, if a member fails to return cards justifying a handicap of 28.0, he may still be allotted an Exact Handicap of that figure at the discretion of the Handicap Committee. However, Affiliated Clubs may always refuse to allot a handicap until a specified standard has been reached.

Alteration of Handicaps

Three definitions come into play here :

(a) The Net Differential is the difference between the nett score returned in a Qualifying Competition and the Competition Scratch Score.

(b) The Competition Scratch Score ("CSS") is a score calculated at the conclusion of each round of a Qualifying Competition, based on a complicated procedure set out in Appendix D in the Scheme booklet, using the Tables in Appendices E & F. The CSS reflects the scores in the competition of Categories 1,2 & 3 players and thus - in theory anyway - whether conditions were more difficult or easier than normal. In extreme circumstances e.g. when nearly all the scores are well above the SSS, the tables will indicate "N/C" which means that the competition is deemed to be abandoned - see Other Handicapping Matters below.

Fortunately there are now a number of computer software packages for recording members' scores and handicaps under the Scheme. Each of these programs will calculate the CSS and handicap adjustments automatically.

All this is a far cry from the old days when the Secretary made his own decision about the SSS for the day.

(c) The Buffer Zone is when the Net Differential is between 0 and a figure varying with each Category - see Summary overleaf. No adjustment to handicaps are made when the player's score is within the Buffer Zone.

If a player's Net Differential is a **negative** figure, his Exact Handicap is reduced immediately (or when the score is notified to the Home Club), by the rates indicated in the Summary below.

If a player's Net Differential is a **positive** figure, and greater than the Buffer Zone, his Exact Handicap is increased by 0.1, either at the end of the month or at such shorter intervals as the Home Club may decide. The Unions may direct (but only the GUI has done so yet) that Exact Handicaps may not increase by more than 2.0 in a calendar year.

SUMMARY

Category		1	2	3	4
Handicap range		5 and under	6 - 12	13 - 20	21 - 28

Buffer Zone
Differentials of   0 to +1   0 to +2   0 to +3   0 to +4

Alterations

		1	2	3	4
If score above Buffer Zone add		0.1	0.1	0.1	0.1
If score below CSS, deduct for for each stroke below *		0.1	0.2	0.3	0.4

Authority of Union or Area Authority to be obtained for

	Clause				
Allotment of handicap	15(4)	Yes	No	No	No
Increase	9(7) & 19(2)(a)	Yes	Yes	No	No
Recommended reduction	19(3)	Yes	To Cat. 1	No	No

Union or Area Authority to be notified on first occasion in any calendar year

Reduction to below scratch	12(6)(d)	Yes	-	-	-

Score returned at Club not Home Club
or at Club of which the player is not a
member can be disregarded   9(8)   No   No   Yes (EGU)   Yes (EGU)
                                               No (Others)   No (Others)

* If a reduction means a player will move into a lower Category, the rate for his present Category shall be used until it brings the *Playing* Handicap into the lower Category, and the rate applicable for the lower Category used for the balance - see Example (2)D below.

EXAMPLES OF HANDICAP CHANGES, assuming the CSS was <u>73</u>.

(1)   *Players A, B, & C each with Exact Handicap of 3.5, Playing Handicap of 4*

	A	B	C
Gross Score	75	78	85
Net Score	71	74	81
Nett Differential	-2	1	8
Change in handicap	-0.2	Nil**	+0.1
New Exact Handicap	3.3	3.5	3.6
New Playing Handicap	3	4	4

(2)   *Players D, E, & F each with Exact Handicap of 20.8, Playing Handicap of 21*

	D	E	F
Gross Score	87	97	107
Net Score	66	76	86
Nett Differential	-7	3	13
Change in handicap	-2.2*	Nil**	+0.1
New Exact Handicap	18.6	20.8	20.9
New Playing Handicap	19	21	21

    * Change of Category (1 x 0.4, 6 x 0.3)   ** In Buffer Zone

Other Handicapping matters

The rules regarding <u>suspension, lapsing and loss of handicaps</u>, and <u>restoration of</u> handicaps, are contained in paragraphs 17 & 18 of the Scheme booklet.

The procedure for the restoration of handicaps following suspension, lapse or loss changed from 1 January 1993. Now, if a handicap of a player is to be reinstated within six months of it being lost, or suspended or lapsed upon the player's suspension from membership of his Home Club, it shall be reinstated at the handicap the player last held. In all other cases, the player has to obtain a handicap by complying with Clause 15, but the Handicap Committee must then still give due consideration to the handicap last held by the player.

Under <u>Clause 19</u> (often known as "Rule 19" within Clubs), the Handicap Committee has powers to increase or reduce a player's Exact Handicap if it considers that his present Exact Handicap does not reflect his general playing ability. Considerations to be taken into account by the Handicap Committee are given in Clause 19(4). The requirement to report such reductions or increases to the Union or the Area Authority are set out in the Summary above.

If a <u>competition is abandoned</u> for any reason, the CSS shall be deemed to be the SSS, and players returning Nett Differentials of less than zero will have their handicaps reduced in the normal way but the handicaps of players with Nett Differentials above the Buffer Zone will not be increased.

The Appendices

Appendix A   An example of the handicap record sheet which has to be kept by the Handicap Committee for each Member.

Appendix B   Table of Handicap Adjustments. A ready reckoner showing the reductions in Exact Handicap at various levels of handicap, with Nett Differentials from -1 to -12.

Appendix C   Table for converting Par and Stableford scores to Nett Differentials.

HANDICAP ALLOWANCES as recommended by CONGU

Notes :   (1) References to Handicaps in all cases refer to Playing Handicaps.
            (2) Strokes to be taken at the holes indicated by the Stroke Index.
            (3) Half strokes count as one.

Match Play

Singles	Full difference in handicap *
Foursomes	One half of the full difference between the combined handicaps *
Fourball	Back marker to concede strokes to the other three players based on three quarters of the difference.

Stroke Play, Stableford, or Par Competitions

Singles	Full handicap
Foursomes	One half of the combined handicaps of the partners
Fourball	Each player receives three quarters of handicap.

* The EGU "sees no reason to depart from the traditional three quarters of handicap" for singles match play but the GUI, SGU and WGU all fully support these recommendations. Handicap allowances in a handicap competition must be laid down by the Committee in the Conditions of the Competition.

When extra holes are played in a knock-out competition, strokes should be taken at the same Stroke Index holes as in the 18 holes.

9
Ladies' Golf and the LGU Handicapping System

This Chapter is about the role of the Ladies Golf Union, its handicapping system, and the various responsibilities of the players, the affiliated Clubs, and the National Organisations involved in ladies' golf.

The Ladies' Golf Union, founded in 1893, has prime responsibility for the administration of ladies golf throughout Great Britain and Ireland. Its **Executive Council**, which meets five times a year, comprises its President, the Chairman, the Hon Treasurer, and two elected councillors from each of the National Organisations of the four home countries. Each of those councillors has an elected deputy who will attend the Council meetings in the councillor's "unavoidable absence".

Beneath the Council there are various other committees and sub-committees viz.

- Finance and General Purposes
- International Selection
- Rules and Regulations Sub-committee
- Scratch Score Committee
- Training Committee.

The Rules of the LGU are set down in *The Lady Golfers Handbook*, published annually by the LGU.

In its Rules, the **objects** of the LGU are stated to be:

a) To uphold the Rules of the game, to advance and safeguard the interests of ladies' golf and to decide all doubtful and disputed points in connection therewith.

b) To maintain, regulate and enforce the LGU system of handicapping.

c) To employ the funds of the LGU in such a manner as shall be deemed best for the interests of ladies' golf, with power to borrow or raise money for the same purpose.

d) To maintain and regulate International Events, Championships and Competitions held under the LGU Regulations and to promote the interests of Great Britain and Ireland in ladies' international golf.

e) To make, maintain and publish such regulations as may be considered necessary for the above purposes.

The LGU's Constitution

This consists of :

(a) The National Organisations viz
  English Ladies Golf Association
  Irish Ladies Golf Union
  Scottish Ladies Golfing Association
  Welsh Ladies Golf Union

each of whom has its own constitution and committee structure. *The Lady Golfers Handbook* contains further information about these four National Organisations, helpfully on different coloured paper, and including details of the County Unions, the affiliated Clubs, tournament results, etc.

(b) Ladies Golf Clubs and ladies sections of recognised Golf Clubs in Great Britain and Ireland, and the amateur annual playing members thereof

(c) Ladies Golfing Societies affiliated to the LGU or National Organisations

(d) Affiliated Ladies Golf Unions overseas

(e) Affiliated Ladies Golf Clubs overseas and the amateur playing members thereof.

The Rules also cover a wide range of constitutional matters, such as the election of its officers, procedures at General Meetings (including some useful standing instructions for General Meetings clearly aimed at ensuring that they do not continue for too long !), preparation of accounts, subscription rates, and the standing orders for the Council and the various committees and sub-committees.

The LGU Handicapping System

The full regulations on the LGU Handicapping System (including the LGU Scratch Score Scheme) are also set out in *The Lady Golfers Handbook* (pages 22 - 46 in the 1994 edition). The following is a summary of the salient features of the system, one which has evolved over the years and which works well in practice.

The chief features of the system are straightforward:

- All handicaps shall be fixed on the basis of the LGU Scratch Score
- Handicaps shall be assessed on scores returned, not on general form
- A player's LGU handicap shall be the same in every Club.

The LGU Scratch Score

This is compiled from the sum of the ratings of individual holes based on the LGU's Rating Table with further adjustments for:

a) the amount of run and
b) course difficulties.

The **Rating Table** gives a rating (i.e. a score to one place of decimals) for each hole, based on its length.

Here are some examples from the Table :

Length in yards	Rating
Up to 100	2.7
101 to 112	2.8
219 to 236	3.5
237 to 254	3.6
255 to 272	3.7
399 to 416	4.5
417 to 432	4.6
561 & over	5.5

Adjustment for the **amount of run** is based on the Table of Course Groups. For example, a course on which the average amount of run (when the carry from the tee is 180 yards) is nil to 5 yards is classified as a Group 1 course for which 2 may be added to the total from the rating table. Where the average run (on the same carry) is 11 - 20 yards, the course is Group 3 and no adjustment is made. Groups 5 & 6 apply on overseas courses only, where the average run is very much further.

The adjustment (b) for the **course value** has to be undertaken by an LGU Scratch Score Assessor. It can vary from -1 to +2 (at 0.5 intervals), according to the difficulty of the course (other than length already taken into account in course rating) and soil, such as

- side hazards e.g. gorse, ditches, trees etc.
- whether the greens are well guarded or open
- whether fairways are wide or narrow
- whether terrain is flat or hilly, or full of awkward stances
- whether the course is exposed to the elements e.g. by the sea.

Examples of Calculation of the LGU Scratch Score

		Course A		Course B
Course Rating		71.4		71.6
Course Group	(2)	+1.0	(4)	-1.0
Course Value		0		+1.0
		72.4		71.6
Scratch Score therefore*		72		72

*Decimal points are rounded up at the end of calculation

A Club may allocate par to a hole, but the handicaps are always calculated against the LGU Scratch Score, not against par. The LGU Scratch Score must be clearly and corrected stated on the Ladies score card of each Club. A Club may not alter or fix the Scratch Score, and the LGU Scratch Score Assessor must be informed of any alterations to the course.

Handicap Categories

Under the LGU System there are five:

Silver Division	Category A	Handicaps 3 and under
	Category B	Handicaps 4 - 9
	Category C	Handicaps 10 - 18
Bronze Division	Category D	Handicaps 19 - 29
	Category E	Handicaps 30 - 36*

A * indicates the handicap has been limited by the application of the regulations.

The Player's Responsibilities and Rights

(a) It is the player's responsibility to know and apply the handicapping regulations, and play off her correct handicap at all times. Handicap certificates must be produced when required. Any reduction in handicap is automatic and comes into force immediately.

(b) An LGU handicap may be held by

- An annual playing member of a Club affiliated to the LGU
- An individual member of either the LGU or the four National Organisations (see above)
- A temporary member of an affiliated Club provided her membership is to last for a period of not less than twelve months.

(c) An LGU handicap may be obtained by submitting four "extra day scores" on LGU affiliated courses with scratch scores of 60 or over. Play must be in twos, i.e. one player per marker. Play must be from LGU tees. If the round is played on a course of which the player is not a member, the card must be countersigned by a local official to certify that the scratch score is correctly stated.

There are other provisions concerning adverse conditions, Society day competitions, etc.

(d) **Calculation of LGU Handicap.** The handicap is the difference between the players actual average score and the Scratch Score of the course, the calculation and rules varying with the five different categories as follows:

Category	Handicap Range	Calculation of Handicap
A	3 and under	Average of differentials from at least ten scores in qualifying competitions, not more than six on the player's home course, and with the remaining four being on at least two other courses
B	4 - 9	Average of six best differentials, scored in qualifying competitions
C	10 - 18	Average of four best differentials
D	19 - 29	Average of two best differentials
E	30 - 36*	Best score for one round only.

There are other provisions covering rounding up and rounding down, and for players moving from one category to another.

(e) **Revision of Handicaps**. On 31 January each year, all handicaps have to be recalculated on the basis of scores in the preceding year, on the formulae outlined above. Handicaps from plus to 34 can only go up by a maximum of 2 strokes, handicap 35 by a maximum of 1 stroke.

The minimum number of rounds to be played to retain a handicap are the same as for calculation of handicap except that there must be a minimum of four scores for categories C, D, and E. Handicaps lapse if this minimum is not met, and the regulations set out the procedure for regaining a handicap which has lapsed.

Other regulations cover Junior handicaps, former professional golfers and membership of more than one Club.

Responsibilities of the Committee of the Affiliated Club

These are

(a)   To ensure compliance with LGU regulations in :
   * The fixing or alteration of Scratch Scores and indications of teeing grounds
   * Starting places
   * Appointment of Handicap Secretaries and issue of Handicap Certificates.

(b)   To run up to sixteen competitions for the LGU Silver and Bronze medals each year

(c)   To provide recommendations and advice on the running of competitions

(d)   To fix the stroke index of the course

(e)   To ensure the Rules of Golf, etc are followed, help to introduce new members to the Rules and etiquette of golf and deal promptly with matters raised with them by the LGU and the National Organisations.

Responsibilities of the National Organisations

These are described under the following headings:
   1.   Scratch Scores
   2.   Handicap Activities

3. Queries
4. Handicapping Stationery
5. LGU Silver and Bronze Medals
6. LGU Gold and Silver Medals
7. LGU Challenge Bowls
8. Australian Spoons (an annual competition)
9. County Golf.

Addresses, telephone & fax numbers

The Ladies Golf Union. Administrator : Mrs E A Mackie.
The Scores, St Andrews, Fife, Scotland KY16 9AT.
Tel. 0334 475811 Fax 0334 472818.

English Ladies' Golf Association. Secretary : Mrs M J Carr
ELGA Offices, Edgbaston Golf Club, Church Road, Birmingham B15 3TB.
Tel. 021 456 2088 Fax 021 454 5542.

Irish Ladies Golf Union. Secretary : Miss M P Turvey
1 Clonskeagh Square, Clonskeagh Road, Dublin 14.
Tel. (010) 3531 2696244 Fax (010) 3531 2838670.

Scottish Ladies Golfing Association. Secretary : Mrs L H Park
SLGA Offices, Room 1010, Terminal Building, Prestwick Airport, Prestwick,
Ayrshire KA9 2PL.
Tel. 0292 79582 Fax 0292 671279.

Welsh Ladies Golf Union. Secretary : Mrs S Webster
WLGU Offices, Powys House, South Walk, Cwmbran, Gwent NP44 1PB.
Tel. & Fax 0633 871622.

10
Greenkeeping I : The Basic Principles

Jim Arthur has written this Chapter on the essential, basic and proven principles of greenkeeping.

These principles have remained unaltered ever since greenkeeping began, despite periodic set-backs and short-lived fads for treatments which breached these principles but did not stand up to the test of time. It is important to define and agree these principles if any programme of course improvement is to be successful. In golf, as in no other sport, the quality of turf on which the game is played is the most important factor and so, therefore, are the constituent grasses.

The same principles apply to the management of every part of the course - green, approaches, fairways and tees alike - but obviously management will vary in intensity in each of those areas. Whilst the principles have never varied throughout this century, the details of management have naturally been markedly amended. The introduction of greatly improved techniques as well as machines, partly as the result of ever-increasing traffic and partly to mechanise work, have not saved staff but have enabled essential operations to be carried out ahead of play, thus improving productivity and eliminating wasted time. Speeding up the work also releases staff to carry out management in other areas of the course which might otherwise be neglected.

Greenkeeping is basically a very simple science, as it is concerned with the management of only one or two species of grasses, the bents (*Agrostis spp*) and the fine-leaved red fescues.

Avoid agricultural methods
The methods of sound, agricultural, grassland husbandry and good greenkeeping are diametrically opposed in every way.

Many of the problems in greenkeeping arise because of the confusion of thought between high production of intensive grassland management on the one hand, and, on the other, the need to retain in greenkeeping those non-productive, wiry-leaved, fine-textured native species which are weeds to agricultural eyes.

It is wrong to recommend agricultural methods to deal with droughted fairways or poor greens, as this will only aggravate the problem by encouraging the invasion of annual meadow grass *(poa annua)*, thus making absolutely sure that the next serious drought will cause the whole fairway to die or the green to suffer severe damage. Then, instead of faulty management being blamed, the damage will be attributed solely to drought.

If the natural grass cover of any of our open spaces in Britain was liable to be killed by drought then half southern Britain would soon be an arid desert and natural grassland would fluctuate through periods of slow recovery to repeated disasters. This, we know, is never true and whilst such fine turf may well bleach with drought, the deep-rooting grasses never die and soon green over with the first rain.

If, however, the physical and chemical status of the soil is altered, e.g. by excessive compaction caused by extra play (especially under wet winter conditions, when there is disproportionate consolidation), uncorrected by intensive aeration; or by unwise manurial treatment which permits drought-susceptible grasses, such as annual meadow grass, to invade; the turf then changes and with it its drought resistance.

Another example of agricultural motivation is the use of perennial ryegrass on golf fairways and tees. It produces, at best, football pitches with a coarse, open, rapidly growing lush turf and it never dies out. The so-called dwarf varieties are not significantly better. Ryegrass was often used in the past, e.g. for divotting fairways and patching tees because it was so cheap. This has left a problem on many links and heathland courses where the wrong seed was used more than fifty years ago on areas of traditional wear such as the walk-off to the next tee, resulting in coarse turf producing conditions equally unsatisfactory for chipping or putting.

To farming eyes ryegrass is useful, but to greenkeepers it is a weed. The true greenkeeping grasses occur on the poorest of land and are characteristic of worn-out pasture or unproductive native turf.

Fortunately, it is possible to change the grass cover on any soil by management. Sadly it is easier and quicker to change it for the worse by bad management than it is to improve poor turf by good management, but it does not take more than a few years at most, if all the problems have been correctly diagnosed.

The change that occurs can be easily demonstrated. Look at the grasses on a pathway across a fine fescue links turf. When soils become compacted, it is always annual meadow grass with the finer grasses being displaced because they cannot compete with surface-rooting annual meadow grass. Look also at the old marking out lines on an abandoned tennis court or across an approach where limed lines have been marked out to restrict the passage of trolleys. The fine, wiry turf grasses have been almost completely displaced along a narrow line by coarser grasses, particularly annual meadow grass, and by worm-casts and weeds, though the native turf immediately adjoining shows none of these undesirable features.

A second cause of bad advice is the fact that so many golfers demand lush fairways and soft, holding greens. The old traditional greenkeeping school aims at producing conditions which are as near to perfection as possible all the year round and not just for a few summer months when growth is at a peak. Lush greens in the summer mean thatchy bogs in the winter and we play golf in this country for many more months under winter than under summer conditions.

A third cause of bad advice is that too many advisers are merely thinly disguised salesmen. There are some competent advisers, e.g. employed by fertiliser companies, but since they correctly advocate minimum use of fertilisers and greater reliance on mechanical than manurial management they are not necessarily better appreciated for being right.

The colour of greens is not important

The first point to stress is that we play golf on fine grasses and not on colour. The chase after colour has caused more problems and consequent costs than almost any other factor. It is interesting to note that the reaction against the "nice and green school" is as strong now in the States as it is in this country.

Clubs must decide whether they want nice greens or green greens - they cannot have both. Fast, fine, firm, true putting surfaces must surely be the aim of all better golfers. Sadly, too, many of the poorer ones (who logically are in the majority in any Club) demand soft, target greens so that their lack of skill in imparting back-spin to a properly struck ball is of less importance when pitching into soft, soggy surfaces.

Lush grassy lies prevent any back-spin being imparted to the ball and the end result is always a flier. Then we hear demands for more water to be applied to the greens to make them hold better. Target golf means the end of all-the-year-round play on to full greens since soft greens in summer are likely to mean temporaries all winter.

Under very dry conditions even the best players may find it difficult to stay on firm greens, but there is no golfing law which states that any player should be able to shower a green with long irons from any angle and always stay on. We should see less of the tarted-up, annual meadow grass dominated, superb putting surfaces presented for one week for a tournament with little regard for the inevitable consequences. Peaks are always preceded and followed by troughs. Annual meadow grass is capable of giving very good conditions under very frequent mowing, but only for a few short months in the summer.

All greenkeeping divides between those (hopefully a minority) who actually want annual meadow grass coupled with a majority who end up with it, often to their surprise and concern; and those, on the other hand, who strive desperately to retain or, even more desperately, to restore the true, native, fine-textured grasses which produce as good golfing conditions in mid-winter as they do in mid-summer.

How to encourage fine fescues and bents

To learn how the desirable grasses can be favoured we must examine those natural environments where fine fescues and bents dominate the native turf. It must be accepted that the vegetative cover of any soil in temperate climes is determined by the soil type - chemical, physical and geological - and the treatment applied to it - natural, e.g. rainfall; or managerial, e.g. fertilisers, mechanical treatment etc. Thus, if the same grasses dominate different environments there must be factors common to all these soils.

Since fine fescues and bents dominate such markedly different ecologies as arid sandy links and flooded tidal salt marshes; acid moors, alkaline chalk downs and limestone heaths; thin, sandy heathland and old worn-out pastures or parkland on heavy soils (if they are well drained) - then logically the common factors which determine the dominance of these grasses cannot be either acidity or alkalinity, soil moisture content or even soil type.

The factors are:

- extreme infertility with virtually all available plant foods either leached out by free drainage or by periodic flooding, or locked up by acidity
- free draining
- unconsolidated, structured soils which favour deep root development.

It has been known for over sixty years that high phosphate levels are essential for the healthy growth of annual meadow grass, permitting it to invade fine bent turf.   The earliest records of research linking high phosphates and annual meadow grass dominance go back to the 1920's and were the basis of the original acid theory, which was designed to lock up phosphates and, thereby, ensure the dominance of bent grasses instead.

The disadvantages of annual meadow grass

As mentioned earlier, annual meadow grass is capable of producing excellent putting surfaces under weather conditions which favour growth provided it is fed and watered generously and mown daily (or even more frequently) but it is the cause of 90% of all greenkeeping problems.   It is an ephemeral, shallow-rooting, prolifically-seeding (even under blades of the mower at closest cut), coarse-textured species, which is very susceptible to drought, disease, wear and winter kill.   It must regenerate from seed and often has only a ten-week life cycle.   Consequently, it looks exceedingly sick at the end of a long period without growth.   All too often this induces a desire to fertilise it and this ensures that the last traces of bents depart.

Above all, annual meadow grass is the most prolific **thatch** producer of all grasses. Thatch is a layer of undecomposed vegetation derived mainly from dead leaves and stems rather than roots, and not to be confused with fibre.   It holds water like a sponge and is often stagnant and waterlogged, even over relatively dry and permeable foundations.   Thatch is always caused by one or more of three factors:

- over-watering, made all too easy by pop-ups
- over-feeding, especially with phosphatic fertilisers
- under-aeration, aggravated by objections to disturbing putting surfaces

All these terms are relative. There is nothing wrong with pop-ups in themselves. Bad design, with heads spaced way beyond manufacturers' maximum recommendations inevitably creates both over-watered, boggy centres, and missed areas on perimeters. If pop-ups are used to make greens hold better, thatch is inevitable. Blame not the pop-ups but those foolishly abusing the ease with which over-watering is made possible.

There is now less over-feeding as fertiliser manufacturers take increasing note of the damage phosphates can do to fine turf. More and more are turning out a standard nitrogen-only mix, based on an equal part mixture of sulphates of ammonia and iron with dried blood and fine hoof & horn meal, which is as old as greenkeeping and is used on most courses in good condition.

Soil analysis

In practice, it has been found that phosphate levels of 7 - 10 ppm are adequate for *Agrostis* and fine fescues, but that annual meadow grass demands minimum levels of 60 - 100 ppm. A check by the STRI on some 1,800 of their soil samples showed less than 1% in the range 10 - 30 ppm and only another 4% between 30 - 60 ppm. All the rest were very high by greenkeeping standards, with an unbelievable 27% so far off the scale that the phosphate was too high to be measured. No wonder annual meadow grass is such a common weed.

Phosphate levels on fairways may often be 10 - 30 ppm with greens on the same course in excess of 650 ppm! Potash is not significant and is hardly needed and it is known that high potash figures inhibit fine fescues.

The acidity (pH figure) is unimportant and the desirable fine grasses grow as happily at a pH of 4.5 as they do at pH 8.5 if other essential conditions are met.

It follows, therefore, that soil analyses are of little value in greenkeeping, as generally they only confirm that manurial levels are far too high.

The need to keep fertility low has been appreciated since the earliest days of greenkeeping. The old methods of feeding links greens a century ago were with soot and sand. Soot is a slow-acting nitrogenous fertiliser and the sand is today generally replaced by a sandy compost.

The Recommended Treatment

All greenkeeping hinges on a few simple treatments, more mechanical than manurial and applying to every part of the course. These are:

- **Aeration** - far more needed now, as there is far more play and consequently more need to correct the resultant compaction. It is the most important of all treatments.

- **Top Dressing** - with humus rich sandy material to produce true playing surfaces, improve resilience, aid drought resistance and provide a slowly available source of plant foods. It is vital that there are no drastic changes in the physical condition of top dressing used, or layering will occur and with it severe root breaks.

- **Mowing** - which must be in two planes, vertical as well as horizontal. Verticutting should not be confused with scarification and should be restricted to the growing season. Nothing speeds up putting surfaces more. The mower is the most important machine in greenkeeping.

- **Irrigation** - which must be restricted and used merely to keep the grass alive, never to make it grow or to make it green and certainly never, never to make greens softer and more holding.

- **Fertiliser Treatment** - this must be minimal. No autumn fertilisers are needed. They merely encourage disease, stimulating grass at the wrong time.

All the rest of greenkeeping is detail. The control of weeds, moss, coarse grasses, pests including earthworms, diseases, etc. will become less necessary as healthier turf is produced. For example, once earthworms are controlled weeds find it harder to invade. Chronic fusarium disease in the Autumn is a sign of bad greenkeeping.

With ever-increasing play it is necessary to carry out more corrective mechanical treatment. The complaint "Can't you leave the greens alone for five minutes?" can only be answered "Yes, if you stop playing on them". Aeration, of course, must be varied in depth to avoid creating cultivation pans. Slitting is the most effective and solid tining the most harmful form of aeration, but which type is employed is immaterial compared with not carrying out aeration at all.

Continuity in management is essential

The biggest problem in greenkeeping today is, however, the lack of continuity, often triggered by frequently-changing Green Committees determined to make their mark in their year of office and by the search for something different for the sake of difference.   Consequently, the history of greenkeeping on any course is all too often one of cyclic deterioration and recovery as fresh generations repeat the follies of their predecessors.

11
Greenkeeping II - Aspects of Course Management

This second Chapter on greenkeeping contains some further basic information on course management.   The references at the end of each section are to the articles on the same subjects which have been published in The Golf Club Secretary *over the past three years (e.g. V1/40 = Volume 1, page 40).   Most of these articles were contributed by* **David Stansfield,** *a senior agronomist formerly with the STRI, now a Director of PSD (Agronomy) Ltd.*

Aeration

The constant trampling of players and the passage of machinery causes the soil beneath the turf to become compacted and this process is the source of the vast majority of greenkeeping problems, because it leads to poor turf and slow drainage. Constant attention, year round, to alleviating and preventing compaction of soil is vital. Such work is unpopular at times, but it simply **has** to be done if the Club is to get maximum use from the course to the best average standard.

[V3/40]

Bunkers

The choice of the right type of sand is important and will vary between inland and seaside courses.   White sand looks attractive but can cause problems with spillage, plugging and splash.   New sand should always match the existing sand wherever possible.   No sand will perform well, though, unless the bunkers themselves are well shaped, well drained and in good condition overall.

[V1/40]

Your Committee may be tempted, from time to time, to move or close bunkers or create new ones but it would be well advised to consult a reputable golf course architect before taking any such action. Consultation is not necessary, though, every time a bunker is rebuilt or modified. Such work is necessary because raking, mowing of margins, climbing of banks, blasting sand out and windblow can all lead to the erosion of the entrances and the faces, loss of definition between turf and sand, and to other damage. Sometimes trimming will be sufficient, but periodically rebuilding the entire bunker will be necessary. This maintenance work must be part of the regular greenkeeping programme.

The style of new or rebuilt bunkers is also important - should they be pot bunkers, splash bunkers or bunkers built into mounds? The design should be consistent with those already on a course and they should be constructed so that they are well drained, easy to maintain and fair on the golfer.

[V1/48]

Course alterations

Clubs should also always consult a reputable golf architect before embarking on changes to the course rather than relying on the ideas of some well intentioned members or of the Club Professional. Many Clubs now have it written into their constitution, or their Golf Course Policy Document (see below), that no alterations can be made without such consultation. In the UK, the architect chosen should be a member of the British Institute of Golf Course Architects (see page 120).

[V4/64]

Disease

It is impossible to eliminate diseases but possible to control them within acceptable limits. Disease is a continuing interaction between the turf, pathogens and the environment (including the weather). The most common diseases on golf courses are fusarium and anthracnose.

Fusarium appears when conditions are damp and humid, especially in the Autumn. It can also occur when excess lime is present, after prolonged snow, or after top dressing. It is important to watch closely for outbreaks and to apply specific treatment rapidly. Preventative spraying is only recommended in special circumstances.

The strategies for the control of all diseases are:

- **Cultural** - using sound turf management practices such as moisture removal, thatch control and controlled fertiliser application.
- **Biological** - cultivating the best grass species available. *Poa annua* i.e. meadow grass is more susceptible to disease than the finer fescues and bents.

- **Chemical** - using pesticides but implemented only when the other two strategies have failed. The proper use of pesticides involves the correct identification of the disease, choice of the most suitable chemical, the judicious use of that chemical, and the timing of the applications.

[V3/56]

Drainage

The results of poor drainage on golf courses during spells of wet weather is all too self-evident. It is important to assess where the water is coming from and why it cannot get away before deciding the remedial action necessary. A common cause of water accumulation is surface water run-off, i.e. when rainwater does not soak into the soil but runs down into the lowest adjacent point. The simple answer then is to install catch-water drains to intercept water running down the slope, if possible in the rough so that the drains need not be covered by turf. Reshaping the ground can be a further way of directing surface water away from putting greens.

Soil compaction is another reason why rainwater is not being absorbed where it falls. The cure for compaction may be vertidraining, blasting with compressed air, using a "Robin dagger", vibratory mole ploughing or mole ploughing, to varying depths, or simply hollow-tining. The problems of surface water can also be due to severe worm-casting or because the old drainage system has become blocked or damaged.

The above reasons, for which the remedies are comparatively straightforward, usually account for about 80% of all drainage problems. For the remaining 20% (where there is, for example, an impermeable subsoil and/or a need to lower the water table and/or spring water) the only way of improving the drainage will be by installing new drains.

It should be possible for your own greenkeeping staff, hiring specialist equipment as necessary, to handle small scale operations. However, if a major new installation is needed, it is wise to seek the advice of an independent draining expert and to have the work done by a reputable contractor.

Whenever new drains are installed it is essential to be clear where the surface water is to go. Soakaways are insufficient unless they can empty from the bottom.

[V4/96 & 104]

Drought conditions

In recent years there has been low rainfall during the summer months and occasionally restrictions on using water for irrigation.

Protecting the greens in such situations is then the priority. The recommended action is :

- Reduce the frequency of mowing to a maximum of three times a week and raise the height of the cut to 6mm.
- Use pedestrian mowers only.
- Put pin positions near the edge of the greens
- Apply light top dressings whilst the grass is still green.
- Avoid the use of all pesticides, fungicides and fertilisers, and the temptation to use a little water if a small supply becomes available.

If, despite these precautions, the brown grass becomes brittle crisp, no play on the greens should be allowed, to avoid permanent damage which will be both lengthy and expensive to put right.

A good wetting agent programme, started in the Spring and kept up whilst the soil remains damp, will help any rain that does fall during a drought to get into and re-moisten the soil which has become dry.

[V1/96]

On fairways, whilst the drought continues, raise the height of cut.

For better protection again future droughts, the recommended action includes introducing drought tolerant species by over-seeding (but not with rye grass), adding extra organic matters as top dressing in the Autumn/Winter after aeration, and routine scarifying in Spring and Autumn.

[V3/40]

Environmental considerations

The environmental objectives on all courses should be to retain the existing landscape wherever possible and to encourage all forms of wildlife which are already in the area.

This will involve the sound management of the rough - whether long grass, heather, dune grassland or woodlands. Some Clubs have even put bird boxes and bat boxes around the course. Ponds which are looked after properly will be an encouragement to many forms of wildlife and a wide range of marsh and marginal flowers and plants.

The environment can also be protected by avoiding the over-use on the course of fertilisers, pesticides and other chemicals, some of which may leach to surrounding areas, as well as being poisonous to wildlife.

New courses often have to be environmentally assessed through a full ecological survey before planning permission will be granted.

[V1/60 & V4/45]

Fairways

The types of machinery available for maintaining fairways has grown tremendously in recent years. Mowers now vary from the traditional trailed gang mowers up to those with hydraulically driven reels and floating cutting units, either mounted on a tractor or as a self-propelled unit. There are also now some excellent scarifiers and machines for aerating.

Although the hydraulic mowers are much more expensive than the traditional gang mower, they do give maximum uniformity of finish over undulating ground, and maintain cutting speed in tight corners or through slow turns. The more expensive machines can produce the striped fairway effect, as seen strikingly at the 1994 Open at Turnberry. It is also possible now to box clippings when fairway mowing.

An economic compromise is to use gang mowers for the majority of the fairways but cutting the approaches to the greens with a triple mower, boxing the clippings if desired. The regular aeration of fairways is essential, using deep slitting regularly during the year and vertidraining the most important or badly compacted areas at least once a year. Scarifying is also highly recommended as a routine task. The divotting of fairways is too often left either to the local Artisans' Club or to the occasional volunteer task force of members, rewarded by a free supper afterwards. Ideally divot holes should be filled at least weekly by a greenkeeper or by another trained person, perhaps a pensioner willing to devote some hours each week to this task.

Worm-casting has become a problem again following the recent banning of chlordane, a remedy which was effective for several years. The pesticides which may be used instead give only a few months' protection. Acidifying the soil will also help control earthworms.

[V4/48]

Greens

The state of your Club's greens will often become a subject for intense discussion amongst your fellow members.

Construction of Greens

The building of a green is a skilled operation and should never be left to inexperienced or amateur contractors. Unless construction is in accordance with the accepted standards in the industry (the "USGA Spec." or equivalent UK version) problems will inevitably arise in future years.

Rapid drainage of greens is absolutely essential and this is achieved by having three layers above the underlying subsoil:

- First, stones of a size and specification which will create an effective void to allow rain water to move freely into the drainage system in the sub-soil
- Secondly, a "blinding" layer of lesser grade aggregate to support the top layer and prevent it from falling into the stones below
- Finally, a layer of root-zone medium in which the grass will grow.

[V2/80]

Mowing

The height of cut should always be decided by the Head Greenkeeper. It is normally within the range 4 - 6mm depending on the condition of the green, the likelihood of drought, frequency of mowing, the type of machine being used and other factors. For special events only and preferably not more than in three separated weeks during the season, an effective 3mm height may be used, provided it does not damage the green and does not cause lining across slopes.

The frequency of cut through the summer should be as to close to daily as possible, on greens in good condition.

The speed of mowing affects the stress put on the grass. Bare patches can occur when turns are too tight.

The choice of machinery lies between pedestrian mower and ride-on-triples. The latter are now used extensively on greens because of the saving in staff time over pedestrian mowers. Most triples also allow verticutting to be carried out. However pedestrian mowers are still also used, particularly in winter conditions and when a more pleasing striped finish is required.

[V3/16]

Thatch

Anyone involved in any way in golf course management will have heard of "thatch" being mentioned as a condition known to affect adversely the performance of a green.

Thatch is an accumulation of organic matter between the surface and the root-zone material (or topsoil) in which it is supposed to be growing. It is a mixture of dead and dying matter (not yet converted into humus) and live plants trying to grow through this layer into the soil beneath. The problem arises when the thatch is so dense that the roots cannot come through, and start to grow sideways, adding further to the thatch layer.

It varies in appearance between an open-structured hard brown crisp material beneath fescue and bent grass turf, to a range of 'greys', to a soggy stinking yellow and black mass which is usually associated with the worse types of annual meadow grass swards. Fibrous thatch, where roots and stems have become woody to protect themselves from erosion and sandy conditions or toxic materials is usually found on fairways rather than on greens. It manifests itself as severe susceptibility to dryness which can be checked by more intensive surface treatments, not by applying lime.

Stagnant thatch, caused when the accumulation of organic matter far exceeds the rate of biological breakdown, is largely self-inflicted. It arrives either because the roots cannot go downwards into compacted soils or into an inhospitable sand layer or because the roots have been encouraged to stay near the surface through the over application of fertiliser and/or water, the latter often through over-enthusiastic use of modern irrigation systems. Poor year-round drainage will also prevent root penetration into the soil below.

The cure for thatch is primarily intensive aeration through slicing, hollow tining, vertidraining, compressed air using a Robin dagger, or the Toro Hydroject - a machine which aerates by injecting very small high pressure water jets into the soil.

[V3/8 and V4/9]

Top Dressing

The application of bulk materials as top dressing should be carried out regularly on the greens, and other closely mown areas on the course.

The dressing used will be a mixture of sand and organic material, the precise mix being selected by the Head Greenkeeper.

Large amounts of top dressing are needed in order to achieve the primary purpose of smoothing out indentations. It should be applied during the growing season but not after September as this risks stimulating fusarium. On greens application should be little and often to achieve the best results. Elsewhere, tees are normally dressed twice a year, perhaps more frequently on short holes. Aprons should require only one application in the Spring.

Topsoil or peat can be put on fairways which need a further layer of humus to stimulate growth.

[V2/88]

Winter Greens

Members dislike playing on temporary greens but they must be reminded that severe damage can be caused if play is allowed on the main greens during adverse weather conditions. The safest policy is as follows :

- When the greens are frosted solid, play may cause no immediate damage but care should be taken if a thaw is imminent or likely.

- When there is a thaw, play must never be allowed as severe damage can be caused.

- Play in other types of bad weather during the Winter will mean that the turf will take longer to revive in the Spring.   It may also cause expensive structural damage to the underlying soil.

- The level damage caused is directly proportional to the level of play.

The Head Greenkeeper should be the person who decides whether play on the greens is to be banned for the day.

[V3/55]

Machinery

Successful course management today requires a combination of skilled trained greenkeepers and the best possible machinery and equipment.

For an average 18 hole golf course, the machinery which is used week in week out is likely to be

- 2 x Triple mowers for putting surfaces
- 4 x Pedestrian operated mowers for putting surfaces
- Triple mower for tees and aprons
- 2 x Pedestrian operated mowers for tees and aprons
- Triple mower for banks
- Gang mower for fairways
- Gang mower for semi-rough
- Mower for deep rough
- Flymos and strimmers
- Compact tractor or Cushman or another ATV
- Fine turf attachments for the above, e.g. top dressing spreaders, aeration equipment
- 2 x Medium - large tractors
- Trailer
- Bucket loader
- Fairway slitter and sweeper
- 200 - 300 litre sprayer.

Other equipment such as scarifiers, vertidrain machines, Hydrojects, etc can be hired if the frequency of their use does not justify a purchase.

A very wide selection of machinery is now available from different suppliers.   You should ask for demonstrations of equipment on your own course and rely on your greenkeepers' opinions thereafter, before deciding on one particular supplier.   Other factors to be borne in mind when making a choice are the availability of optional extras, spares, the guarantees offered, dealer back-up, and cost of servicing.   Machinery using diesel rather than petrol engines are noisier but cheaper to run.

Many Clubs now spread the cost of new and replacement machinery by planning their purchases over a rolling, five-year budget and/or entering into leasing agreements.

[V2/72]

Policy Document

A Golf Course Policy Document is strongly recommended.   It should set out in detail

- The objectives of the Club's course management policies

- The roles and responsibilities of those involved
- Resources of staff, machinery and materials to be made available
- The standards of upkeep required on each area of the course (tees, greens, fairways, bunkers, rough, woodlands, etc.)
- Procedures for closing the course
- Other matters such as financial control (including preparation of budgets), ecology and outside professional advice
- A Code of Conduct on the lines of the following example :

Code of Conduct on the Course for Members, Visitors and Green Staff

1. The Green staff normally require four hours to complete the daily course preparation work. They start at 6.30 am in summer, at daybreak in winter. Players starting before 9 am in Summer are asked to give priority to the Green staff, to enable the work to be completed as early as possible.

2. Green staff when working on an area during the remainder of the day will stand aside when necessary, after signalling when they are ready for a ball to be played towards them.

   Players are asked to ensure that they do not play shots which may endanger the Greens staff working near or ahead of them.

3. Notices will be put up in the Clubhouse when chemicals are being used on the course, if special tasks such as vertidraining are being carried out, and if any temporary greens or tees are being used.

4. Any complaints must be made to the Secretary, not to the Green staff. The Secretary will look into the complaint and refer it to the Committee if it is of sufficient importance.

It is most important that the Policy Document should be agreed and approved by members, preferably at a special meeting held to discuss the course. Once the Policy Document has been approved in this way, it avoids any future arguments and discussions about the way in which the course is being maintained. Obviously it is desirable that its content are reviewed on a regular basis.

[V4/36]

Rabbits

Now that rabbits have become immune to most forms of myxomatosis, they have become a menace again on many golf courses, causing unsightly damage to tees and fairways.

The best methods of controlling them remain either shooting, or gassing (by a specialist contractor).

Building a wire mesh fence all round the perimeter of the affected area can be effective, but is an expensive solution. The fence has to go under the ground a certain depth to prevent rabbits burrowing underneath.

Other methods are using ferrets or, on a badly infested area, an old lengthy piece of pilchard seine netting to trap them.

[V1/95]

Soil analysis

Root zone soil analysis as a way of determining an effective turf management programme needs to be treated with some caution, as warned in the previous Chapter.   It is an inexact science as the results achieved have to be related to the condition and the type of turf present, the root zone material, the availability of irrigation, the local climate, the previous management programme, and any known changes over a period. The results can also vary according to the season and to the measuring and extracting techniques used.

On greens in the UK, analysis is likely to show an excess of nutrients rather than a deficiency.   Low phosphate content rarely seems to cause problems in practice. Turf on most greens appears to thrive when a good amount of potassium is available, so it is worth checking on the content of that chemical every 3 - 5 years.

[V4/40]

Spraying

The effective use of spraying equipment is now an important part of course management.   Important points to remember are:

• The operator must be properly trained and possess the necessary certificates

• Only **approved** pesticides or fertilisers must be bought, stored and used

- Using the right equipment will enable the task to be done quickly. Most Clubs will have their own 300 litre sprayer attachment to a tractor or ATV, for use on limited areas. When there is a need to spray fairways it is worthwhile employing a specialist contractor who has the appropriate large-scale spray equipment. Very small areas can best be treated using knapsack sprayers.

- More fertilisers are now becoming available in liquid form for use in spraying equipment. Although this is a quick and easy method of applying fertiliser, it should not entirely replace traditional fertilisers in powder or granular form.

[V4/88]

Tees

If tees are to stand the rigour of frequent play, they must be a sufficient size - say up to 450 square metres of usable area on a short hole. To encourage the grass to grow, there should be an adequate depth of root zone material (say 150mm firmed), good access to light and air, and no trees surrounding the tees.

The routine management of tees should include :

- regular mowing, preferably three times per week in the growing season, with clippings boxed off, and usually to a height of 10-12mm

- using fertiliser and irrigation to sustain steady growth and recovery from wear and tear during the Spring and Summer

- moving tee markers at regular intervals, according to the weight of play experienced

- narrowing the teeing area between the tee box and marker, so that it can be changed sideways as well as up and down the tee

- regular, rapid divotting

- applying top dressing periodically

- returfing when major renovations are required.

The use of separate, special tees during the winter months will save wear on the main tees and, if they are planned away from the normal teeing area, will also reduce traffic damage. If the use of winter tees materially reduces the length of most holes it is worth having a special winter score card printed, with an amended SSS.

[V4/24]

Trees

Trees seem to be liked by golfers, especially on inland courses where they can help to determine strategy on a hole and enhance the landscape.

Too many trees, though, around tees and greens will severely affect the growth of the grass and encourage diseases such as fusarium. Constant cutting back and pruning in these areas is essential. One American course superintendent has given his chainsaws the names 'Thunder' and 'Lightning' so that when members query why a tree near a green has suddenly been cut down, he can blame it on either of these two causes !

Planting trees which are unsuitable for a golf course seems to happen all too often. The species chosen should always match those found naturally on the course, and should preferably be of a type which would also benefit the local ecology. Nothing looks worse than an unnatural row of leylandii or poplars, or too many flowering species, all of which make the area look more like a garden of remembrance than a golf course. Too many trees will also affect the natural development of gorse and heather.

Roots from trees can also be a menace when mowing, and cause damage to the drainage system if trees are planted on top of or near drain runs.

[V3/64]

Trolleys and Buggies

The banning of trolleys during winter months is never popular with members ! However even wide-wheel trolleys (now usually the only type allowed on the course) can cause damage by skidding - which causes smearing - and, more importantly, by focusing traffic routes on holes. The diversion of traffic on to alternative routes may not be easy on some holes. In bad weather conditions, the damage caused by trolley users can be long-lasting.

Potentially, buggies can cause more damage than trolleys unless special tracks for them are provided on the course (rare in the UK). If a few buggies are permitted, the users should be encouraged to drive down the edge of the fairways, rather than in the light rough. They should not be allowed to zig-zag nor to go within say 10 metres of a green or on routes between bunkers guarding greens.

[V2/56, V3/32]

Turf

The criteria for ensuring that the right turf is purchased for use on a golf course are:

- **The quality and condition of the grass.**

- **Freedom from weeds, pests and diseases.**

- **The age of the turf.** Ideally it should be about 15 months old, with a thatch area not exceeding 5 mm.

- **The underlying soil** should be as close as possible to the material forming the rootzone on which it is to be laid. Turf with a silt or clay base should be avoided.

- **The choice of the supplier.** You are recommended to visit the field where the turf to be purchased is growing and/or to get samples to compare with the actual delivery.

Re-turfing can now be a very rapid process when it is laid by a contractor using a special machine holding a giant "Swiss roll" of turf.

[V4/120]

Verticutting and Grooming

Verticutting as the name implies means vertical cutting. It is an extra mowing operation which should be carried out not less than once a fortnight on greens during the growing season. It takes out the edges between different clumps of grass thus giving extra trueness and pace by improving texture. It also acts as a mild scarifier by removing material which might otherwise build up into thatch.

Verticutting is a skilled task if damage to certain parts of the green is to be avoided. It should not be undertaken until the marks of the previous verticut have disappeared, normally a period of only 3 - 4 days.

Groomers are in effect mechanical combs fitted into the mowing heads. They also improve texture and will reduce the need for verticutting to a degree but must never replace verticutting altogether.

[V4/128]

Vertidraining

This is a method of aerating greens and fairways, carried out using a special machine which will thump solid tiles into the soil up to a depth of 10-12 inches and give a kick on the tine at its full penetration.

Water features

These are tending to appear more on golf courses, particularly on those constructed recently.   Although often attractive, they require positive management to sustain the visual appeal, and to conserve the wildlife in the water margin.   It is worth remembering that they will be costly to maintain as well as to construct.

Pollution of the water with chemicals is not usually a problem on established courses.   The amounts of pesticides and fertilisers applied are far less than the quantities likely to be put on the land by local farmers.

Siltation must be remedied by digging out or dredging the affected areas.

Terrestialisation is a gradual menace which needs to be checked to ensure that a clear distinction between the course and the water itself is maintained.   Algal bloom and aquatic weeds can normally be treated by spraying with herbicides, after taking specialist advice.

Oxygen starvation caused by acid water can be cured by removing plant litter, and in serious cases by adding chalk.   In larger ponds, aerating fountains are often used to add oxygen to the water.

[V4/32]

Water supply

In recent years, when there have been serious droughts and subsequent bans on the use of mains water supplies, many Clubs have been considering the possibility of having their own supply by drilling a bore hole into sources of water below the course.   Such drilling is not permitted without a licence and the National Rivers Authority now only grant these rarely.

If the NRA advises that a licence may be given, the next steps are to

- Ask the British Geological Society to undertake a survey to confirm that sufficient reserves of water do exist below the course

- Appoint a well known firm of well-borers to carry out the test drilling and other formalities which will be required by the NRA before they grant a full licence.   The cost of drilling can be anything from £1,000 upwards, depending on the depth needed to find sufficient water.

The principal and important advantage of having your own water supply is that it is vastly cheaper - as little as 10% of the cost of mains supply. Having your own bore hole is not a guarantee of uninterrupted supplies, as in times of drought the NRA can still put a temporary ban on extracting water from it.

A licence from the NRA is also needed before water can be abstracted from rivers, dykes, etc within the course.

Winter Course Management

The use of winter tees and the banning or re-routing of trolleys have already been mentioned. Using artificial tee mats - now much better in design and feel than they used to be - and temporary greens in adverse weather conditions will also help minimise the damage caused by winter play. Preferred lies should also be introduced during the winter months.

Maintenance between October and December should include repairs to all the damaged areas, which should then be clearly protected from golfers trampling on them by hoops rather than by white lines.

[V2/56]

Quality sums it up

Larry Gilhully of the USGA Green Section, in an entertaining talk at a BIGGA Education Conference in 1991, said that he had discovered that the desirable attributes of a successful greenkeeper and the undesirable features found too often on golf courses can be summarised under the word QUALITY in

Desirable in a Greenkeeper

Qualified
Unflappable
Accessible to members (and able to able to Address them)
Leader
Intelligent
Teacher (or Trainer)
Yeoman (willing to work with his staff on the course)

Undesirable features of golf courses

Quagmires (bad drainage)
Unnecessary compaction
Atrocious soils
Lousy irrigation
Inadequate Inventory control (of machinery and materials)
Trees (too many)
Your expectations as a member are too high.

12
Golf Clubs and VAT: The New Regime

The VAT legislation applicable to most Members' Golf Clubs changed significantly during 1994. This Chapter explains those changes and how they will affect the finances of a Members' Golf Club. Some other VAT topics are also covered.

Registration and accounting for VAT

Any organisation, including Golf Clubs of all kinds, has to become registered for VAT if its annual "taxable supplies" (i.e. sales or income) exceed a certain figure (£45,000 since 1.12.93). Organisations making taxable supplies below that limit, unless they request to be registered, do not have to charge VAT @ 17.5% on their standard-rated supplies, nor can they claim back any VAT they have paid on purchases.

VAT has to be accounted for quarterly (or monthly by option). A Club therefore has to pay over to HM Customs and Excise ("Customs") within one month of the end of each VAT quarter any VAT it has charged on its income ("output VAT") but may deduct from that sum that part of the VAT paid to its suppliers ("input VAT") which it is allowed to recover. If the recoverable VAT exceeds the output VAT in any quarter Customs will repay the difference within about a fortnight of receiving the quarterly return.

The position prior to the changes

VAT had to be charged on all the income of a Golf Club registered for VAT, except the few items which are normally exempt under VAT law (e.g. interest receivable, rents receivable, etc). Thus VAT had to be added to entrance fees, subscriptions, green fees, bar and catering sales and income from gaming machines. However the Club, being registered for VAT, was able to recover **in full** all the VAT it paid on all its purchases - from wines and spirits to the most expensive course machinery.

Is VAT Irish?

Clifford Joseph, an early speaker on VAT when it was introduced in the UK in 1973, always used to point out that

- **Input** VAT is VAT you pay **out** to your suppliers

- **Output** VAT is VAT you get **in** from your customers

- **Exempt** or **partially exempt** organisations are the only organisations registered for VAT which actually **pay** VAT. The others can recover all their input VAT in full.

The background to the changes in the legislation

After many months of lobbying by the CCPR (Central Council of Physical Recreation) and others, the Government was persuaded in 1993 that the application of VAT to amateur sports had been illegal under the Sixth and Eighteenth EC Directives since 1 January 1990. An announcement to this effect was made by Sir John Cope in Parliament on 22 July 1993.

Discussions between HM Customs and Excise representative sporting bodies began in earnest in September of that year. A Consultation Paper was issued by Customs in October 1993 on which comments were invited. This was followed by an Information Paper and draft Treasury Order in February 1994, in which Customs outlined their proposed changes in more detail. The new legislation - introduced by Treasury Order - finally came into effect on **1 April 1994,** but importantly was back-dated to **1 January 1990.** Advice on its application can be found in a helpful Customs' *VAT Notice 701/45/94,* issued in May 1994. This leaflet includes a list of the 114 sports which at present qualify for exemption, ranging from aikido to yoga, and including baton twirling (?), snooker, billiards and pool. Bridge and other card games are not on this list.

These changes only apply to non-profit making organisations ("NPMOs"). For Golf Clubs this definition means Members' Clubs which do not distribute their profits or surpluses in any way to their members or to a third party, but retain them for the general benefit of their membership. The VAT position of Proprietary Golf Clubs and Clubs run by local authorities remains unchanged, though the position of the latter is currently under review. The term Members' Clubs for the rest of this Chapter refers to Clubs which qualify as NPMOs.

Some Members' Clubs with constitutions of limited companies with share capital have standard Articles of Association, often based on Table A of the relevant Companies Act, which permit dividends to be paid. Providing no dividends or other profit distributions have ever been made, Customs have indicated that they are prepared to accept that such Clubs still qualify as NPMOs. It is advisable though, to amend the Articles as soon as possible to preclude any possibility of distributions in the future.

The changes for Members' Clubs

Exempt and standard-rated supplies

For Members' Clubs the following supplies are now **exempt** from VAT (Note 1) :

- Entrance fees
- Subscriptions (& levies), other than social and non-playing
  subscriptions (Note 2)
- Green fees paid by
  - five day members playing at weekends or by
  - members who pay a low annual subscription plus an amount each
    time they play
- Trolley hire (if by the Club) to members
- Locker rents
- Billiard/snooker money-in-the-slot charges to members.

b) The following supplies remains **standard-rated** for VAT purposes :

- Subscriptions from social and non-playing members (Note 2)
- Green fees paid by all visitors, and by members for their guests
- Bar and catering sales
- Gaming machine income
- Trolley hire (by the professional)
- Billiard/snooker money-in-the-slot charges to visitors

Entrance fees to competitions are sometimes standard-rated, sometimes exempt - see page 91 below.

Note 1   There is an important distinction in VAT law between exempt supplies (i.e. sales) and zero-rated supplies. Zero-rated only applies to a few categories of supplies such as sales of food (but not catering), printed matter like books and newspapers, young children's clothing, etc. If part of your income is zero-rated and the rest is standard-rated, there are no restrictions on the amount of your input VAT which you can recover.

But - as explained later in this Chapter - if part of your income is exempt, you are unlikely to be able to recover all your input VAT.

Note 2 Customs reserve the right to apportion playing subscriptions between exempt and standard-rated supplies if the non-playing element is significant e.g. if a Club provided free food to its members in return for a higher playing subscription. If a Club wishes to apportion its social subscription which carries the right to play snooker, it will then have to apportion all its subscriptions.

The effect of these changes is that Members' Golf Clubs have now become partially exempt for VAT purposes, no longer able to recover all the input VAT they have paid unless they can take advantage of what is known as the *de minimis* rule, which is explained below.

How much input VAT can they recover?

A partially exempt organisation has first to analyse its input VAT in three ways :

(1) Input VAT on purchases relating to supplies which are standard-rated, all of which is **wholly recoverable**. In Golf Clubs, this will include VAT on bar and catering purchases, on gaming machines costs, and on any expenditure directly attributable to the bar, kitchen and dining-room areas.

(2) Input VAT on purchases directly attributable to supplies which are exempt, **none of which is recoverable** unless the *de minimis* rule applies - see below. Such purchases will be rare in most Golf Clubs but will include items such as new lockers for members, signwriting members' honour boards, and repairs to the members' trolley storage shed.

(3) All other input VAT, i.e. that relating to supplies which are both standard-rated and exempt, only part of which may be recoverable. In a Golf Club, therefore, this residual VAT will apply to most expenses e.g. on the course, on the house and administration.

Fortunately the advent of computerised accounting software does enable this analysis of input VAT to be made easily, entry by entry.

A partially exempt organisation may then recover:

(a) all the input VAT wholly attributable to taxable supplies ((1) above), **plus**

(b) a proportion of the residual input VAT ((3) above) using either the *standard* method, or a *special* method previously agreed with Customs, to calculate that proportion.

However if the input VAT directly attributable to exempt supplies ((2) above) plus the irrecoverable residual input VAT is less than £600 per month on average, the *de minimis* rule applies and **all** input tax then becomes recoverable.

Standard method

Under the standard method, which is comparatively simple and has much to commend it, the proportion of residual input VAT recoverable is

- Total of taxable supplies, divided by total of all supplies, rounded **up** to the next highest percentage.

Investment income and rental income can be excluded from the total of all supplies, and the sales of capital goods (other than motor cars) must be excluded from both figures in this fraction.

Special methods

As a general rule, these are worth considering if the Club's taxable income is low, or its exempt income is high, compared with its total income. For example, a *special* method which a Golf Club might find worth adopting is as follows:

- VAT on Course expenses : the recoverable proportion is the number of rounds played by visitors, divided by the total number of rounds played by both members and visitors.

- VAT on Clubhouse expenses : the recoverable proportion is the floor area devoted to the kitchen, bar and dining room activities, divided by the total floor area.

- VAT on administration expenses : the recoverable proportion is based on the proportion of time spent on work associated with taxable supplies.

Some other special methods are mentioned by Customs in their *Notice 706 - Partial Exemption.* Your Club's accountants may have suggested another which is particularly beneficial to your Club. No rounding up is allowed of percentages calculated under a special method - presumably to encourage more use of the standard method.

EXAMPLE of a calculation under the **Standard** method and of some VAT planning points which arise:

MARVIS BAY GOLF CLUB — Year ended 31 March 1995

Income	Exempt £	Standard-rated £
Entrance fees	10,000	
Playing subscriptions	230,000	
Social subscriptions		10,000
Green fees from Societies etc		125,000
Green fees from 5 Day members for weekend play	10,000	
Catering sales		80,000
Bar sales		90,000
Investment income	3,000	
Fruit machine income		5,000
Totals	£253,000	£310,000

Input VAT

Attributable to taxable supplies	20,000
Attributable to exempt supplies	500
Residual - routine expenses	15,000
- new mower (March 1995)	3,500
Total	£39,000

Recoverable percentage of Residual Input VAT

£310,000 / £560,000 = 55.36%, rounded up to 56%.

Input VAT Summary	Recoverable	Irrecoverable
Attributable to taxable supplies	20,000	
Attributable to exempt supplies		500
Residual - 56% of £18,500	10,360	
- 44% of £18,500		8,140
Totals	£30,360	£8,640

VAT Planning points

(1) If the purchase of the £20,000 mower had been deferred until April 1995, the irrecoverable input VAT would have been reduced by 44% of £3,500 = £1,540, bringing the total exempt input VAT down to £7,100 - just below the *de minimis* average of £600 per month or £7,200 per year. All the input VAT would then have been recoverable.

(2) If the Club's catering had been "franchised out", the proportion of residual input VAT recoverable would have been reduced to £230,000/£480,000 = 47.92%, rounded up to 48%. The recoverable input VAT would then have been £1,480 less - not a significant sum in itself, unless the addition puts the total exempt input VAT over the *de minimis* limit.

(3) Increases in taxable income will increase the proportion of residual input VAT recoverable. This perhaps strengthens the argument for introducing a bar/catering levy system (see Chapter 15) to boost spending by members in those two areas.

The annual adjustment

The above calculations of recoverable input VAT have to be made quarter by quarter, when the VAT returns are submitted. An *annual adjustment* is worked out at the end of the quarter following the end of the Club's VAT year, at which time any over or under recovery of input VAT has to be settled with Customs with the VAT due that quarter.

VAT Planning Point (4)

If it can be arranged that the bulk of the exempt income of the Club (i.e. entrance fees and subscriptions) is received in the final quarter of the Club's VAT year, more residual input VAT can be recovered in the first three quarters, with cash flow advantages for the Club.

Claims for the period prior to 1 April 1994

You are no doubt aware that the backdating of the new VAT regime to 1 January 1990 has resulted in most Members' Clubs being able to reclaim substantial sums of VAT from Customs, being the VAT wrongly charged on subscriptions, entrance fees, etc. less the input VAT over-recovered because previously partial exemption rules did not apply. The estimate of the total refund due to all Sports Clubs varies from the government's figure of £40 million to others of up to £150 million.

Some points worth noting about this refund:

- The starting date for the period for which a reclaim is being made can be any date after 1 January 1990 but must be for a continuous period to 31 March 1994.

- Clubs have to analyse their past years' VAT returns quarter by quarter separating out standard-rated and exempt supplies, and analysing input VAT in the three categories mentioned earlier.

- Interest will be payable by Customs. There is no deadline by which repayment claims have to be submitted. The interest can amount to 20% or more of the refund claimed.

- Some complex extra statutory transitional relief is available to ensure that no Club will pay more VAT (as a result of the change in the law) on major projects completed between 1 January 1990 and 31 March 1994, or contracted before 1 April 1994 and completed before 31 March 1999.

- If a Club would owe more VAT to Customs under the new legislation for the period 1 January 1990 to 31 March 1994, it need take no action, the legislation simply coming into effect from 1 April 1994.

The Members' rights to share in this refund

There has been much debate, both amongst members and in the media, as to whether members have a legal right to their share of the net VAT refund received by the Club. Many members feel they should, on the basis that the Club was merely acting as agent, collecting the VAT from the member and passing it on to Customs. Counsel for the National Golf Clubs' Advisory Association has expressed an Opinion that the Club has no legal right to retain the net refund.

This right to share in the refund was subsequently challenged, however, in an article in *The Golf Club Secretary* by a solicitor, and by an Opinion by Andrew Park QC given to the CCPR. The main reasons given for these opposing views were that (a) the Club was liable to pay the VAT and not the member, (b) the member was charged VAT under a mistake of law not a mistake of fact, and (c) there is no implied term which binds the Club to make refunds to members.

It seems therefore that the legal position will not be certain unless and until the matter is resolved through the courts. As mentioned in an earlier Chapter, a member cannot sue his or her Club if it is constituted as an unincorporated Members' Club, because the members are the Club and vice versa, but can if it is a limited company. (Past members can sue, of course).

The Committees of most Members' Clubs - and indeed a majority of their members - appear to be in favour of the Club retaining the refund, perhaps using it to repay borrowings or to embark on special projects which might otherwise be delayed. The calculations of each Member's share of the refund would be a tedious exercise, but not impossible if records of subscriptions and entrance fees paid by members during the refund period are readily available.

The *moral* argument for crediting each member and his or her share of the net refund is that it is the fairest method, especially if it is one which takes into account the length of membership and the amount paid during the refund period.

The Effect of the New Legislation

Members' subscriptions in the future

This will clearly vary from Club to Club, depending upon the proportion of input VAT recoverable. In the example given earlier in this Chapter, the non-recoverable input VAT of £8,640 which is an additional expense for the Club represents just under 4% of subscriptions so that - other things being equal - the amount of subscriptions paid by members could be reduced by 17.5 - 4%=13.5%

Irrecoverable VAT on expenditure

As a Committee Member you need to be aware, therefore, that each time the Committee authorises the purchase of some expensive course equipment, it is likely that x% will have to be added to the cost for the irrecoverable VAT on the purchase.

Increasing taxable income

When considering the merits of 5 day members versus Societies, remember that, if your Club is using the standard partial exemption method, each pound of extra taxable income i.e. green fees means a little more input VAT can be recovered, however illogical this may seem.

Raising substantial funds for major projects

Before these changes came into effect, a Club raising funds by way of shares or loan notes which carried inter alia the right to reduce subscriptions for the holders could find itself liable to account for VAT on that benefit. There were several Court cases to determine whether and to what extent VAT was payable. In Members' Clubs, as subscriptions have become exempt from VAT, this VAT liability has ceased. Offering a restricted number of life memberships now becomes an attractive and simple way for a Members' Club to obtain additional funds for major projects.

Other VAT Matters

Competition entrance fees and VAT on prizes

The VAT applicable to these items is complex. The basic rules are:

- The entry fee is exempt if the competition is for members only and all the fees received are spent on prizes.

- The entry fee is standard-rated if the competition is open also or solely for non-members, or if the entry fee includes a supply which is normally standard-rated e.g. lunch and/or tea.

- The entry fee may be apportioned between exempt and standard-rated if it includes a standard-rated supply of goods or services not normally available to non-competitors e.g. the gift of an umbrella.

On prizes VAT has to be accounted for whenever a prize worth £10 or more is distributed i.e. as if a sale had then taken place. Many Clubs instead adopt an alternative method under which they do not claim input VAT back when purchasing prizes costing £10 or more. Customs will accept this alternative, simpler procedure.

[V3/4,10]

Gratuities

Compulsory gratuities, such as charges to Societies, are standard-rated, but voluntary gratuities e.g. donations by members to the staff Christmas fund, are outside the scope of VAT.

VAT accounting date

The Club's quarterly accounting date and its VAT year end may be altered by agreement with its local Customs office, provided a reason for change is given. Cash flow advantages can sometimes be achieved by making these alterations.

Junior subscriptions

Some Clubs have found it financially worthwhile to establish with their local Customs office that, from the start of VAT (1 April 1973), subscriptions paid or payable by their members aged 21 years or less, fell within the exemption given to services provided by Youth Clubs or Associations. Certain conditions about its Youth section have to be met to achieve the saving. For Members' Clubs, of course, young members playing subscriptions have become exempt from 1 January 1990.

Rents

Rents for the use of land for sporting activities for more than 24 hours are exempt from VAT. However a landlord can elect to waive this exemption usually because he (the landlord) being partially exempt wishes to convert an exempt supply into a taxable supply for VAT purposes. A Members' Club which is partially exempt, should always try to discourage the landlord from exercising this option.

13
Other Taxation and Business Rates

Golf Clubs are subject to other forms of taxation besides VAT, notably corporation tax and the uniform business rates levied by local authorities.

Corporation Tax

Operating surpluses

Proprietary Clubs are treated like any other trading company and so are liable to pay corporation tax on their annual profits as computed in accordance with the tax laws.

Members' Clubs - whether incorporated or not - do not have to pay corporation tax on their annual surpluses, provided these surpluses are retained within the Club for the benefit of members generally. This important concession arises because the surpluses arise from "mutual trading" between the members and the Club (which is the members in effect or legally).

However, in recent years, more Golf Clubs have been approached by their local Inspector of Taxes, seeking corporation tax on the profits made from **trading with non-members** i.e. visitors other than members' guests. A few seaside holiday courses with large green fee income have been paying corporation tax on this profit for some years. The Revenue's view was clarified recently by the following announcement in the August 1994 edition of the Inland Revenue Bulletin :

> *SCHEDULE D, CASES I & II: TRADING RECEIPTS OF MEMBERS' GOLF CLUBS*
>
> *We have been asked whether non-proprietary members' golf clubs are liable to tax on trading income such as visitors' green fees. This article gives our view on when income received by members' Clubs for the use of their facilities by non-members is taxable trading income.*
>
> *Any surplus arising to a members' Club from transactions with its members is not normally taxable. Payments by members in respect of*

their personal guests even when these are described as "visitors' fees" are normally regarded as part of that surplus.

But receipts from visitors who, in return for payment on a commercial basis, are allowed to use a Club's facilities will be receipts from a taxable trade in the Club's hands. This applies to individuals who arrive at a Club to use its facilities on a casual basis and to groups who may book in advance.

Such visitors may become "temporary members" of the Club. But this will not prevent receipts from their use of the Club's facilities from being taken into account for tax unless their rights as temporary members (such as rights to vote at meetings, participate fully in club activities and generally to exercise control over the running of the Club), and the opportunities to exercise them, are similar to those of full members. In computing the taxable income derived from non-members in this way the related expenses will be deductible, including a reasonable proportion of course overheads.

The new "Pay and file" system for corporation tax does place greater responsibilities on organisations to disclose their taxable income, with penalties for failure to do so.

Because of these recent developments, your Club would be well advised now to discuss this possible liability to pay corporation tax with its auditors (or failing them with a professional adviser specialising in this field). It is often possible to produce a computation acceptable to the Inspector of Taxes which shows that little or no profit arises from visitors after deducting the appropriate expenses from green fees.

Investment income

All Clubs have to pay corporation tax on their investment income and interest receivable. It is important to make certain that interest receivable is paid gross as any income tax deducted at source cannot be recovered by the Club.

Capital gains

Corporation tax may also be payable on capital gains made when a Club sells certain assets viz. land, buildings, mineral and other rights, paintings, objet d'art, shares and other investments. The rules on the computation of the taxable gain are complicated and professional advice should always be obtained when such a sale is contemplated.

[V2/91]

Uniform Business Rates (UBR)

Golf Clubs are liable to pay UBR in the same way as other businesses, but most will have been enjoying the transitional reliefs introduced when the UBR came into operation in 1990.

Under Section 47 of the Local Government Finance Act 1988, local authorities do have the power to give non-profit making sports Clubs further relief on their UBR burden. Unfortunately, this relief seems usually to be granted only to small Clubs like village cricketers and not to Members' Golf Clubs, presumably because local councillors feel that the latter are wealthy enough to pay the UBR in full.

[V5/12]

There will be another revaluation of all commercial properties with effect from **1 April 1995**. As the rateable value is based on the hypothetical rent of the property, the recent sharp increase in rents being paid by Golf Clubs since recent rent reviews is likely to have an adverse knock-on effect on the new rateable values.

It is worthwhile, therefore, trying to ensure that your Club's rateable value is not overstated, by seeking expert advice from a chartered surveyor with experience in acting for Golf Clubs. All occupiers are likely to have only six months in which to lodge an appeal. Based on previous experience, it may be several months, if not years, before the appeal is settled with the local Valuation Officer.

[V5/1]

Other taxes

Golf Clubs are liable to pay **stamp duties,** and the two new taxes coming into effect in 1994 - on **general insurance premiums** and **air travel** (if any).

14
Health & Safety

The Committee is primarily responsible for ensuring that the Club complies with Health and Safety legislation. Failure to do so can invoke penalties of fines or imprisonment or both.

This Chapter contains a general introduction to the subject, an overview of the most important current legislation, some examples of health and safety risks which can occur within a Golf Club, and a summary for Committee members, with recommendations. Information about how copies of the books or leaflets mentioned in the text (and marked *) can be obtained is given at the end of the Chapter.

Introduction - Management of Health and Safety
(reproduced in full from the HSE's booklet *Health and Safety in Golf Course Management and Maintenance** by kind permission of the Controller of Her Majesty's Stationery Office)

Health and safety within any workplace needs to be managed and controlled to ensure that good standards are maintained and, where necessary, improved. The effective management of health and safety is key in preventing accidents and ill health at work.

Competent management systems include:
- setting a clear health and safety policy which covers the selection of people, equipment and materials, the way the work is to be done and what is required to do it safely;
- assessing the risk of certain hazards and practices found in the workplace
- ensuring that adequate preventative measures are in place to control certain hazardous conditions and procedures
- training staff in safe working practices
- monitoring and reviewing those working practices, and
- effective communications with all those involved in managing and maintaining the golf course.

Responsibilities of the Club

Golf Clubs are normally managed by a Committee [or Council] supported by a number of sub-committees. As part of the management of health and safety, the Committee would be responsible for ensuring that:

- employees and members are familiar with the Club's safety policy and the arrangements to implement it
- all employees are competent and trained and aware of the hazards in carrying out their duties
- safety equipment and devices are properly used and maintained
- machinery and equipment are properly maintained and safe to use
- working practices are regularly reviewed to improve health and safety.

Training and Competence

Training is one way of achieving health and safety competence and helps to convert information into safe working practices. Accident statistics show that many accidents occur when employees use machinery, equipment or substances without proper training and instruction.

All employees, including senior management, will need some training and information about health and safety. New employees (including volunteers and casual staff) should receive induction training on health and safety, including on how to operate machinery safely, using pesticides, emergency procedures, fire and evacuation. Also, a risk assessment may identify groups of workers especially at risk, such as young people and those employed on a casual basis for short periods each week, e.g. caddies.

The competence of staff should be monitored, especially as lack of job knowledge and skills can adversely affect health and safety. Any necessary update or refresher training should be provided. Special attention may need to be given to employees who deputise for others. Their skills are likely to be underdeveloped and they may need more help in understanding how to work in a safe and healthy way.

Further information and advice on training can be obtained from:

- the Greenkeepers Training Committee
- local Training and Enterprise Councils who will be able to provide advice on National Vocational Qualifications (in Scotland, local Enterprise Companies and Scottish Vocational Qualifications)

- Agricultural Training Board - Landbase
- National Proficiency Tests Council
- Colleges of further education

It is most important that a record is kept of all training, whether "hands on" internally by the Club's staff or from attendance on external courses.

The Legislation

The Health and Safety at Work etc Act

The volume of legislation on health and safety has grown rapidly in the last twenty years, since the passing of the *Health and Safety at Work etc Act 1974* ("The H&SW Act"). *Tolley's Health and Safety at Work Handbook 1994** lists no less than 45 Acts or regulations now in force !

The H&SW Act placed a general obligation upon employers, so far as is reasonably practical, to:

- provide and maintain machinery, equipment, appliances and systems of work that are safe and without risk to health
- ensure that articles and substances are used, handled, stored and moved safely, again without risk to health
- maintain a safe place of work
- provide and maintain a working environment which is safe and with adequate welfare facilities
- provide information, instructions, training and supervision to ensure the health and safety of all employees
- ensure that they and their employees carry out their work so that contractors and other visitors are not exposed to health and safety risks
- if they employ five or more persons, prepare a written statement of their health and safety policies, revise it regularly, and bring to the attention of all their employees.

The H&SW Act also established (a) the Health and Safety Committee (HSC) giving it power to propose health and safety regulations and Approved Codes of Practice (ACOPs), and (b) the Health and Safety Executive (HSE) as the unified executive arm of the HSC responsible for enforcing health and safety laws. That enforcement and inspection responsibility has now been delegated to environmental health officers employed by local authorities.

The H&SW Act is still very much in force and remains the principal legislation on which most of the subsequent Acts and Regulations are based.

The "Pack of Six"

Six new regulations, known as the "Pack of Six", came into force on 1 January 1993 (or later as noted below). These are based on EC directives and "flesh out" the general provisions of the H&SW Act and consolidate or replace other UK legislation already in force. The six were:

1. *Management of Health and Safety at Work Regulations 1992 ("The Framework Regulations")*
2. *Personal Protective Equipment at Work Regulations 1992 ("The PPE Regulations")*
3. *The Provision and Use of Work Equipment Regulations 1992 ("The Work Equipment Regulations")*
4. *The Manual Handling Regulations 1992 ("The Manual Handling Regulations")*
5. *The Workplace (Health, Safety and Welfare) Regulations 1992 ("The Workplace Regulations")*
6. *The Health and Safety (Display Screen Equipment) Regulations 1992 ("The VDU Regulations")*

Some sensible, down-to-earth advice on complying with these regulations is given in a book *Health and Safety Are You at Risk**. It also contains the full text of the six regulations.

1. The Framework Regulations

These are intended to improve existing health and safety management by requiring employers specifically to :

- make and record the assessment of **all** foreseeable health and safety risks within the organisation (but excluding trivial risks or risks arising from routine or general activities unless they have special relevance to the organisation)

- make arrangements to introduce preventative measures shown by those risks assessments to be necessary

- review the risk assessments regularly

- establish and implement procedures to be followed when anyone at work is in serious or imminent danger. Such procedures should cover, for example, the orderly evacuation of the clubhouse in the event of fire.

- take in account their employees' capabilities (as far as health and safety are concerned) e.g. previous experience, knowledge and training

- appoint a competent person to implement the measures needed to comply with the legislation. The degree of competence is not defined, but the ACOP published with the regulations gives some helpful advice to employers as to whether or not an employee can be considered as competent.

2. The PPE Regulations

These require employers specifically to ensure that suitable personal protective equipment is provided **and used** by employees at all times.

3. The Work Equipment Regulations

These pull together previous regulations governing the use of equipment at work. For "existing equipment first provided for use" before 1 January 1993 some of the regulations apply from 1 January 1993, some not until 1 January 1997. For equipment new *to the Club*, all the regulations apply from 1 January 1993 .

These regulations require *inter alia* that the work equipment must be suitable and appropriately maintained, and that specific risks relating to each machine are identified. Proper information, instructions and training must be made available.

4. The Manual Handling Regulations

These are aimed specifically at reducing the large number of injuries and accidents at work caused by employees and others wrongly handling loads, (not necessarily always heavy loads). They supplement the H&SW Act and the Framework Regulations. Employers are required to review all their manual handling activities and if possible to discontinue those where there is a risk of injury. Where a manual handling task has to be undertaken, employers must make a more detailed risk assessment and introduce the appropriate preventative measures to minimise the risk of injury.

There is also the usual duty on employers to provide information (such as the weight of a load) to employees engaged in manual handling which involves a risk of injury.

5. *The Workplace Regulations*

These both supplement the general requirements under the H&SW Act and consolidate previous regulations. They set out in greater detail how employers can ensure that they provide a place of work which is safe and without risks to health. Premises built after 1 January 1993 or modified thereafter must comply with the Workplace Regulations immediately. Other premises have to comply from 1 January 1996.

Aspects of the workplace which under these regulations require attention include:

- maintenance
- ventilation
- temperature
- lighting
- cleanliness and disposal of waste
- room dimensions and space
- workstations and seating
- traffic routes
- dangers from falling objects or steps
- windows, doors, gates, etc. (and ability to clean windows safely), and
- the provision of washing, toilet facilities, drinking water, lockers, and areas in which to change, rest and eat.

6. *The VDU Regulations*

These put further responsibilities on employers, for an area of work activity not previously covered by other health and safety legislation. They apply (or will apply) to all VDU workstations , whether manned by an employee or by self-employed person working for the organisation, unless the use of the VDU is incidental. They come into force immediately for new workstations on or after 1 January 1993 and by not later than 31 December 1996 for installations put into service before or on 31 December 1992.

The specific duties for employers laid down in the VDU Regulations are to :

- assess and review the health and safety risks to persons exposed at VDU workstations and to reduce the risks identified

- comply with the comprehensive requirements for VDU workstations set out in the schedule to the Regulations. These cover not only the display screen, the keyboard, the work desk or work surface and work chair, but also the environment within the office

- plan work routines for employees so as to provide breaks for those at present using the VDUs all day

- provide at regular intervals free eye and eyesight tests for employees using a VDU, if asked to do so

- provide training and information for the VDU users.

Other Legislation between 1975 and 1990

COSHH

The *Control of Substances Hazardous to Health Regulations 1988* ("COSHH") came into force from 1 January 1990. Under it, the main duties of employers to their employees are to :

- carry out and review a formal independent assessment of the health risks to employees of all hazardous substances at work (see definition below*) and thus determine the precautionary measures needed

- ensure through control systems that those precautionary measures are implemented properly. This would include the use of the appropriate PPE

- provide health surveillance when necessary

- provide information and training regarding the transport, storage and use of the hazardous substances.

* **"Hazardous substances at work"** include

- those which are classified as very toxic, toxic, harmful, irritant or corrosive

- other pesticides, cleaning agents and oil

- wood or other dust, perhaps created by a process being carried out

- those present in a particular environment e.g. where rats are present or where there are open water courses.

It is recommended that COSHH assessments are made in writing and reviewed regularly.

Control of Pesticides

The *Control of Pesticides Regulations 1986* cover the sale, supply, advertisement, storage and use of pesticide products, which include fungicides, herbicides, insecticides, public hygiene pest control products, rodenticides and wood preservatives.

Only approved pesticides should be stored and used, under the conditions printed on the product label (as stated in each pesticide approval). The rules regarding the safe storage of pesticide are also stringent.

Noise at Work

The *Noise at Work Regulations 1988* were introduced to reduce hearing damage caused by loud noise. They require employers to take appropriate preventative action e.g. providing ear protectors when the noise exposure levels reaches 85 dB (A) "First Action Level" or above. As a first step, however, efforts should be made to reduce the noise levels.

First Aid at Work

Under the *Health and Safety (First Aid) Regulations 1981*, all workplaces are required to have certain first aid material in a clearly identified box. Some modifications to the regulations were included in the ACOP on first aid (*First Aid at Work**) published in July 1990 e.g. extra items (such as a bottle of eye wash) can now be added to the contents of first aid boxes. A trained person or persons must be appointed to administer first aid on or off the course.

Reporting of Accidents and Incidents

Certain injuries which occur at the workplace or as a result of work activities are reportable under the *Reporting of Injuries, Diseases and Dangerous Occurrence Regulations 1985 ('RIDDOR')*. A helpful checklist of those which are reportable, and those which are not, is given on page 7 of the HSE's booklet *Health and Safety in Golf Course Management and Maintenance*.

The incidents to be recorded should include all known near misses by flying golf balls. Any accident or incident which occurs should always be investigated fully to determine the action needed to prevent a recurrence.

Food Safety Act 1990

The main aims of this Act were to :

- continue to ensure that all food produced for sale is safe to eat and not misleadingly presented
- strengthen existing legal powers and penalties
- keep pace with technological change.

Most of its provisions came into force on 1 January 1991, others at later dates by subsequent regulations.

The principal offences under the Act are :

- selling, or possessing for sale, food which is injurious to health, unfit for consumption or contaminated
- rendering food injurious to health
- selling food which is not of the nature, substance or quality demanded
- falsely or misleadingly describing or presenting food.

All food premises (such as Golf Clubs providing catering) were required to be registered with their local authority between 1 February and 1 May 1992. Local authorities, through their trading standard officers and environmental heath officers (EHOs) are primarily responsible for enforcement of the Act. Both categories of officers have power to enter food premises if they are investigating possible breaches of the law, and may also take away samples of food.

If an officer believes a food business is not complying with hygiene or food processing regulations, he may issue an **improvement notice,** requiring the proprietor to put matters right. It is possible to appeal against such a notice.

Failure to carry out the remedies required under the improvement notice may lead to prosecution by the local authority. If successful, the Court may issue a **prohibition order**, closing the business down wholly or partially, if it considers there is a continuing risk to health. In extreme cases, an officer can issue an **emergency prohibition notice**, and then apply to the Court for an **emergency prohibition order** to be made. Lifting of a prohibition order can only be made on application to the Court, after a period of six months (or three months after the previous application).

The penalties for food offences have been increased under the Act and can be heavy fines and/or imprisonment.

In practice, EHOs have sometimes made unreasonable demands and in those circumstances it is worth going to appeal. One of the most famous examples was at the Thurlestone Hotel in Devon, where the EHO required two separate knives to be used when making up ham and tomato sandwiches - one for the ham, the other for the tomato. When redesigning kitchen areas it is always advisable to call in the local EHO at an early stage, before plans are finalised.

Electricity at Work Regulations 1989

These set new standards for the maintenance and use of electrical equipment in the workplace. The chief responsibilities falling upon an employer are :

- electrical systems and electrical equipment within the employer's control should be installed and maintained by a competent person, so as to prevent danger to any user of them.
- Portable equipment (including cables and plugs) should be regularly checked and maintained. A safety isolating transformer or residual current device should be used when operating hand-held equipment out of doors.
- Battery charging should be carried out in well-ventilated rooms.
- Employees must be reminded about the possible dangers from overhead power lines and from digging into live cables.
- Adequate training in the use of all electrical equipment should be provided.

Examples of health and safety risks in Golf Clubs

Injuries can arise from(or illness can be caused by) situations such as :

On the course

- Driving tractors or other machinery on steep slopes or too near water
- Using hover mowers incorrectly on steep banks
- Inexperienced staff using chainsaws, post hole borers and similar other specialised equipment
- The misuse of other course machinery e.g. spikers, rotary mowers, groomers, scarifiers etc, including the removal of safety guards or the selection of the wrong machine for the task to be undertaken
- The incorrect storage, transport and application of chemicals such as

fertilisers, fungicides and pesticides, including failing to wash or shower properly afterwards
- Maintenance work on sprinkler systems
- Gassing or shooting rabbits
- Incorrect manual handling e.g. when unloading supplies or trying to move heavy mowers
- Failure to wear the correct PPE
- Fire hazards from petrol spillage, or from the build-up of grass and other debris around the engine/transmission areas which may then absorb fuel or oil
- The build up of dust
- Accidents involving ATVs and similar transport
- Accidents associated with grinding and other equipment in the greenkeepers' sheds
- Flying golf balls, especially at blind holes or where a footpath or road crosses or adjoins the course.

In the Club's premises
- Food hygiene precautions inadequate
- Floors slippery after cleaning
- Wrong use of toxic cleaning materials
- Machinery hazards in the professional's workshop
- Inadequate fire precautions, such as lack of sufficient fire extinguishers, fire exits not clearly marked and insufficient evacuation training
- Poor facilities for handling beer barrels and other heavy deliveries.

Generally
- Trip hazards though untidiness, in all areas - a very common risk
- Faulty electrical equipment/wiring
- Not following procedures laid down for the use of electrical equipment
- Contractors who visit the Club regularly not being made aware of the Club's health and safety policies
- Insufficient warnings to other visitors about possible hazards
- First aid kits not properly maintained. No competent person available to administer first aid
- No formal agreement with the professional as to whether he is producing his own health and safety policy statement, etc., or whether he undertakes to come within the Club's policies
- Inadequate training and supervision of staff.

Summary for the Committee member, with recommendations

You will have realised from reading the previous pages in this Chapter that the sheer volume of health and safety legislation in this country (and indeed in the EC) is now daunting, but that some of it overlaps. You may feel that bringing your Club up to the necessary standards may well take months if not years.

Remembering that it is the Committee who is legally responsible for complying with this legislation, where should the Committee begin ? Here are some **recommendations** on the action it should consider taking, if it has not done so already :

1. Invite an expert Health and Safety consultant to visit your Club for a day, talk to the staff, tour the entire area, and then produce a report on what in his view needs to be done, and the tasks which need to be given priority. He should also be able to help with the production of written COSHH assessments as he should be familiar already with most of the hazardous substances in use on the course.

2. Appoint one member of the Committee to have specific responsibility for health and safety matters within the Club. His principal task will be to ensure that the Club's written health and safety policy document is reviewed and updated regularly, and that the staff are fully aware of its contents. He should also monitor that the policies are being followed in practice. The HSE leaflet *Writing Your Health and Safety Policy Statement** is a helpful guide.

   Ideally he should also aim to produce, with the help of the Secretary and other senior staff, a comprehensive Health and Safety Manual for the Club, comprising :

   - the Club's policy statement
   - the COSHH and other assessments, recording the preventative action taken
   - a record of staff training undertaken
   - minutes of meetings held to discuss health and safety in the Club.

3. Ensure that the prime responsibility for carrying out the Club's health and safety policies is delegated to the Secretary, and through him to the other senior members of the staff.

4. Arrange for the Secretary and all the staff to receive the appropriate training.

5. As soon as some progress has been made, invite your local Health and Safety Inspector to visit the Club. Explain your plans to him, and seek his advice also on the areas of operation which should have priority.

6. Have health and safety policies on the Committee's agenda at least once a year.

Finally keep everything in perspective. If your Club is well managed, it will already be pursuing many excellent health and safety policies, and perhaps little more needs to be done except improving the formal documentation.

* Health and safety publications mentioned in this Chapter

Tolley's Health and Safety at Work 1994
Published by Tolley Publishing Co Ltd., Tolley House, 2 Addiscombe Road, Croydon, Surrey CR9 5AF.
Tel. 081 686 9141. Price £49.95 ISBN 0 85459 745 X.

Health and Safety Are You At Risk ?
Published by CCH Editions Ltd., Telford Road, Bicester, Oxfordshire OX6 0ND.
Tel. 0869 253300. Price £24.95 ISBN 0 86325 317 2.

Health and Safety in Golf Course Management and Maintenance
Published by the HSE. Available from the Greenkeepers Training Committee, Aldwark Manor, Aldwark, Alne, York YO6 2NF. Tel. 0347 838640. Price £9 ISBN 0 7176 0689 9.

First Aid at Work
Available from HSE Books. Tel. 0787 881165. Price £4 ISBN 0 1188 5536 0.

Writing your Health and Safety Policy Document
Available from HSE Books. Tel. 0787 881165. Price £3 ISBN 0 7176 0424 1.

15
Within the Clubhouse

This Chapter is about the clubhouse - its design, maintenance and the activities which take place within it.

Design and maintenance

The advice of **Jim Bell**, of JMB Associates, an architect who specialises in clubhouses and is a speaker at many conferences or courses for Golf Club Secretaries, includes:

- The minimum size of a new clubhouse offering the usual facilities is c. 8,000sf, which means a building cost in the region of £800,000.

- It is essential to have a regular maintenance survey of all the Club's premises, identifying the areas which need attention in the short, medium and long term.

- Refurbishment should be continuing process.   He advises, for example, against buying carpets with a life expectancy of over 10 years, as fashions change.

- Flexibility in the use of space is desirable.   Traffic routes should also be taken into consideration when changes are being contemplated.

- Extensions with flat roofs will prove expensive to maintain.

- An old central boiler can often be replaced with smaller local units, with consequent savings.

- A secure room for the storage of members' clubs plus small lockers for personal items, will take up less space than traditional lockers.

- The increasing requirements of Health and Safety and similar legislation must always be borne in mind (see Chapter 14).

- Never appoint a member as the Club's architect or surveyor, in case things go wrong subsequently.

- Have a trusted local builder for all routine repairs.

Security of premises and the adjoining carparks is a growing problem. Solutions include CCTV cameras both outside and inside, burglar alarm systems, and locks requiring a security number to be entered or the insertion of a "smart card" (see below).

Evacuation procedures in the case of a fire must be clearly understood and if necessary rehearsed by the staff. Having detailed plans of the clubhouse readily available will prove useful if a major alteration is being considered or if rebuilding becomes necessary because of fire or storm damage.

Catering

A survey carried out amongst GCS subscribers in 1991 indicated that:

20% of Clubs ran their own catering with no profit share to the steward/stewardess

6% ran their own catering with a profit share

46% gave their steward/stewardess a catering 'franchise'

28% used outside caterers, occasionally on a profit sharing basis.

More Clubs towards the North of England appeared to franchise their catering out.

Both in-house and franchise arrangements can be equally successful in providing a first class catering service to both members and visitors. The gross profit percentage before staff costs is normally in the range of 50-60% but staff costs usually absorb that gross profit.

As explained in Chapter 4, changing from an in-house arrangement to one involving outside caterers or a franchise to a steward or stewardess (or vice versa), is likely to fall within the Transfer of Undertakings legislation.

There appears to be a growing demand for snack meals to be available at all times of the day, from breakfasts for Society visitors onwards.

A TV set in the snack bar, however objectionable this may be in principle, has been shown to increase sales, especially when a major sporting event is being televised.

Bar

Bar prices can be a bone of contention with members. Some Clubs have a policy of ensuring that their prices are close to those available in local pubs.

The bar gross profit percentage usually averages around 45%, perhaps less on beer and spirits and more on wines and some soft drinks.

Controlling Bar and Catering, and Levy systems

Many Clubs have now installed electronic tills which record precise details of each sale going through the bar and dining room. The information is used both to check the daily takings in the tills, and to provide input data for the Club's bar stock control systems. The success of these tills does rely on the accuracy with which the staff key in the information.

Electronic tills systems can also be adopted to take a "smart card" to enable a Club to introduce a voluntary or compulsory **levy system** under which all members other than the minor categories are required to spend £x on food and drink in the clubhouse during a subscription year. Members are then usually given a discount on the Club's normal prices when they use their smart card. Levy systems used to be instituted by issuing vouchers to members, but this is not a recommended method as accounting for the vouchers is a very tedious job, both for the Steward and for the Secretary.

[V2/84]

A monthly bar stock check and report by an independent specialist is surprisingly inexpensive and a further safeguard to ensure that malpractices are not taking place amongst the bar staff - such as placing their own bottles of spirits on the Club's optics.

Renewing the Club's Licence

A Club must possess a Club registration certificate or a Justices' licence if it wishes to serve alcoholic drinks on its premises. Most Clubs opt for the former as it has certain advantages over the Justice's licence, and only requires renewal normally every ten years instead of annually.

No reminders are given that a Club registration certificate is due for renewal, so a diary note needs to be made of when the present licence expires.
The procedure to renewal is straightforward. Application for renewal

should be made to the local Clerk to the Justices at least 28 days before the licence is due to expire. Renewal can be refused if:

(a) The Club's rules do not (or no longer) comply with the Licensing Act 1964. These are set out in Schedule 7 of the Act, and include the requirement that at a general meeting voting must be confined to members and all members entitled to use the Club's premises must be entitled to vote and have equal voting rights, except that

- The rules may exclude from voting by members below a specified age (not more than 21), or by women in a primarily men's Club or vice versa. Primarily is not defined.

- Members of a person's family who are only members of the Club through a family membership scheme may also be excluded, but not the person taking out the subscription.

[There is another exception relating to Ex-Service Clubs which will not apply to Golf Clubs]

(b) The Club's premises do not comply with standards required by the local fire authority, or if the local police object to the renewal.

(c) The magistrates are satisfied that "the premises are not suitable and convenient for their purpose in view of the character and condition and of the size and nature of the Club".

Renewal of the Club's licence should not be a problem. It seems that, as attitudes change, more and more Clubs are giving their Lady and 5 Day members voting rights.

[Supp. June 1993]

16
The R & A, the Home Unions, CONGU and the USGA

There are a bewildering number of Associations involved in golf, some would say too many. This Chapter explains the roles played by each of the main governing bodies.

The Royal and Ancient Golf Club of St Andrews

Since 1897, the R & A has become recognised as the governing authority for golf in all countries, except the United States and Mexico which come under the United States Golf Association ("USGA") - see below. It enjoys a similar world wide status as the MCC in cricket.

The R & A has three separate and clearly defined functions:

(1) International
(2) National
(3) Club.

(1) International functions

(a)   The Rules of Golf

The R & A is the governing authority on the Rules, both in the UK and for over 60 countries and associations which are affiliated to it. The only other governing authority on the Rules is the USGA.

The Rules are administered by a Committee comprising twelve members elected by the R & A and up to twelve others from golf authorities throughout the world such as CONGU (see below), the USGA, European Golf Association, Asian Pacific Golf Confederation and the Japan Golf Association.

A conference takes place every four years with the USGA to discuss proposals for changes to be made. However the Rules are under constant review during those four years, so that possible improvements can be fully considered before the final conference. An interim meeting takes place with the USGA two years after the last conference, at the time the Walker Cup is played in the United States.

There is also a Decisions Sub-Committee to answer questions from Clubs (**not** from individuals), and from affiliated Unions and Associations. Decisions made are reported annually in *Decisions on the Rules of Golf*, a publication from the R & A and USGA (see page 38).

(b)   Implements and Balls

A separate smaller Committee, working chiefly with, but independently to, its counterpart within the USGA, is responsible for interpreting the Rules and Appendices relating to the control of the form and make of golf clubs and of specifications for the golf ball, set out in Appendices II and III to the Rules of Golf. This is an important task, to prevent the traditions of the game and long established courses being spoilt by technical developments. The complete banning of a certain type of groove from 1 January 1996 is a recent example of action taken by this Committee.

(c)   Rules of Amateur Status

These are the responsibility of a further Committee comprising similar representatives to those on the Rules of Golf Committee.

The procedures for revising these Rules is much the same as those for the Rules of Golf, and no changes are made without due consultation with the affiliated Unions, the USGA and PGA.

This Committee also deals with applications for re-instatement of amateur status, controls scholarships and other grants-in-aid, and answers questions both on amateur prizes, tournament conditions, etc and from individuals about their own position under the Rules.

(2) National functions

The R & A is now responsible for organising :

- *The Open Championship* - a mammoth task in itself. The success of this event, both as a championship and financially, now provides substantial sums which the R & A devotes through its External Funds Committee to the development of junior golf, greenkeeper training, greenkeeping research and other similar causes which benefit golf generally. The prize fund for the 1994 Championship was increased to £1,100,000.

- *The Amateur Championship*
- *The Boys Championship* (since 1948)
- *The Youth Championship* (since 1963)
- *The Seniors Amateur Championship* (since 1969)
- *The Senior British Open Championship* (from 1991 in conjunction with the PGA European Tour).

(3) Club functions

As a private Club, the R & A has a maximum of 1,800 members, 1,050 resident in GB and Ireland, 750 elsewhere. It does not own a course but it is closely involved with the St Andrews Links Trust in maintaining all the four golf courses at St. Andrews, over which it enjoys certain playing rights.

The R & A also supplies one of each of the two joint Chairmen and Joint Secretaries of the World Amateur Golf Council which organises all World Amateur Team Championships. International conferences are held at appropriate intervals to ensure that full liaison is maintained with all the governing bodies and associations from the UK and overseas.

Secretary : Michael F Bonallack OBE. The Royal and Ancient Golf Club of St Andrews, Fife, Scotland. Tel. 0334 472112 Fax 0334 477580.

The Home Unions and CONGU

There are four Home Unions

    (1) The English Golf Union
    (2) The Golfing Union of Ireland
    (3) The Scottish Golf Union
    (4) The Welsh Golfing Union

plus   (5) The Council of National Golf Unions ("CONGU").

(1) The English Golf Union

The EGU, founded as recently as 1924, divides its activities into eleven areas:

(a)   Championships, including the English Amateur and Stroke Play Championships, the County Championships, International matches and other competitions such as the Champion Club Tournament of England.

(b)   Handicapping via CONGU (see below).

(c)   Golf Development.   A separate department assists developers, planners and others in all aspects of golf development and aims to be the recognised co-ordinating body of the country.   There is a network of County Union Field Officers who support this work by their own help and local knowledge and advice.

(d)   Golf Course Committee, formed in the late 1980's to help Clubs with the maintenance of their courses.   During the last three years its seminars throughout the country for Chairmen of Green, Head Greenkeepers and Secretaries have been appreciated and well supported.

(e)   Coaching, through County Unions selecting leading players from their Clubs for coaching through their own schemes, and by national coaching available for up to eighty players over eight regions.

(f)   Advisory Service, answering large numbers of enquiries on topics connected with Men's Amateur Golf in England.

(g)   Individual Membership Scheme, open to golfers who have been elected members of a Club General Committee and/or have held important positions in Clubs or County Unions.

(h)   Amateur Golfer, the official EGU magazine reporting on EGU and County activities and various other aspects of the game.   Circulation is around 13,000 copies per month.

(i)   Insurance both for Clubs and individuals.

(j)   A Society scheme through which a member of a Society who does not possess a Club handicap can be given an EGU registered Society handicap which, although not equivalent to a CONGU handicap, is some indication of his skill at the game.   The scheme was introduced also to help Societies achieve recognition through registration through the EGU. Details of all registered Societies are sent to affiliated Clubs quarterly.

(k)   EGU Membership cards, now issued by many Clubs to their members, and which enable a Club to recognise immediately the golfing status of a visitor.   The card is intended to act as a passport both in this country and at Clubs whose Federation is a member of the European Golf Association.

Secretary : Paul M Baxter. The English Golf Union, 1-3 Upper King Street, Leicester, LE1 6XF. Tel. 0533 553042   Fax 0533 471322. *Amateur Golf* is published by Fore Golf Publications Ltd. 129a High Street, Dovercourt, Harwich, Essex CO12 3AX. Tel. 0255 507526   Fax 0255 508483.

(2) The Golfing Union of Ireland

Founded in 1891, its objects include :

- arranging Amateur Championships, Inter-Provincial and Inter-Club competitions, and International matches
- securing via CONGU a uniform standard of handicapping
- providing advice and assistance (other than financial) to affiliated Clubs on all golfing matters
- generally to promote the game in every way, when this can be done better by the Union than by the individual Clubs.

Administration is via Provincial Councils in each of the four Provinces (elected by Clubs within those Provinces), who nominate a limited number of delegates to attend the annual meeting of the Union.

Secretary : Ivan E R Dickson.   The Golfing Union of Ireland , 81 Eglinton Road, Donnybrook, Dublin 4. Tel. 010 353 1 2694111   Fax 010 353 1 2695368.

(3) The Scottish Golf Union

Founded in 1920, its objects include :

- fostering and maintaining a high standard of amateur golf in Scotland
- administering and organising generally amateur golf in Scotland
- arranging an Amateur Championship, a Scottish Open Amateur Stroke Play Championship and other competitions and matches
- applying the CONGU SSS and handicap system throughout Scotland.

Its organisation is based on sixteen Area Committees, elected by local Clubs in each area.   The Area Associations or Committees elect one delegate each to serve on the Union's Executive.

Secretary : John W Hume.   The Scottish Golf Union, 181a Whitehouse Road, Barnton, Edinburgh EH4 6BY.   Tel. 031 339 7546   Fax 031 339 1169.

(4) The Welsh Golfing Union

The WGU, formed in 1895, is an association of Golf Clubs and golfing organisations.   Its objects include :

- taking steps which may be deemed necessary to further the interests of the game in Wales

- holding a Championship meeting or meetings each year
- encouraging Inter-Club, Inter-County and International matches and such other events as may be authorised by the Council
- applying the CONGU SSS and handicapping system
- assisting in the establishment and maintenance of a high standard of greenkeeping.

The country is divided into ten districts which return a total of 22 members on the WGU's Executive Council.

Secretary : Richard Dixon. The Welsh Golfing Union, Powys House, South Walk, Cwmbran, Gwent NP44 1PB. Tel. 0633 870261   Fax 0633 871837.

(5)   The Council of National Golf Unions ("CONGU")

Created in 1924, its Council comprises two members appointed from each of the above four Home Unions and one member from the R & A. A liaison representative from the European Golf association is invited to attend Council meetings. Any person acting as Chairman of the Council who is not already a member shall be an additional member of the Council.

Under its constitution, its purposes and functions are :

(a) to consider and advise the National Unions on all matters connected with the game of golf
(b) to undertake such further duties and to exercise such further functions as shall be allotted to it from time to time by the four National Unions
(c) to act as a Consultative Committee between the National Unions and the R & A.

Its responsibilities include :

- maintaining and reviewing the Standard Scratch Score and Handicapping Scheme (see Chapter 8)
- nominating two members on the Board of Management of the Sports Turf Research Institute (see next Chapter)
- managing the annual Amateur Home International matches between England, Scotland, Ireland and Wales.

Hon. Secretary : Alan Thirlwell . The Council of National Golf Unions, 19 Birch Green, Formby, Liverpool L37 1NG. Tel. & Fax 0704 831800.

The United States Golf Association ("USGA")

The USGA, formed in 1894, is the national governing body of golf in the United States and Mexico.   Its single most important goal is said to be "preserving the integrity and values of the game".

The USGA has wider responsibilities than the R & A. In addition to most of the functions of the R & A mentioned earlier in this chapter the USGA also

*   develops and maintains the national system of handicapping
*   works in turf grass and turfgrass management i.e. greenkeeping
*   has sections for Seniors, Ladies and Juniors (Boy and Girl).

It has a formidable list of standing Committees covering all the above and other subjects.

17
Other Organisations involved in Golf

As a Committee member, you should also be aware of the following organisations. Those relating to Lady golfers were covered in Chapter 9.

The Association of Golf Club Secretaries

Its aims and objectives are

- To act as an employment bureau, offering help to Secretaries in gaining positions, draft contracts of employment, etc
- To provide training via courses for existing and potential Secretaries
- To provide an information service based on the queries submitted to it by members
- To hold regional meetings and seminars. These invariably include golf after lunch
- To maintain contact with other golfing bodies, the Inland Revenue, HM Customs, etc
- To publish and distribute *Golf Club Management*, a monthly journal, to all its members.

The Association also has a benevolent fund for members and next of kin who need assistance.

Membership is only open to Secretaries who have been in office for at least six months, to National, County and District Secretaries and by invitation to others involved in Golf Club management. Membership may continue after retirement.

Secretary : R E Burniston. 7A Beaconsfield Road, Weston -Super-Mare, Avon BS23 1YE. Tel. 0934 641166 Fax 0934 644254.

British Institute of Golf Course Architects

The main object of this Institute is to encourage the highest standard of golf course design and construction, in the best interests of its members' clients. It maintains a register of members, each of whom has to be fully qualified by training and experience.   It also aims to support research and development into golf course design, construction and maintenance, and arranges meetings and conferences to further its objectives.

Secretary : Mrs S Furnival. The Pheasantry, Tandridge Golf Club, Oxted, Surrey RH8 9NQ Tel. 0883 712072   Fax 0883 730376.

British Association of Golf Course Constructors

BAGCC's objects are

* To promote the development of the golf course construction industry
* To ensure a high standard of work by its members through agreed contractual procedures and codes of practice
* To provide an information service
* To promote training and education of people in the industry.

Hon. Sec. : T J Banks. 2 Angel Court, Dairy Yard, High Street, Market Harborough, Leics. LE16 7NL. Tel. 0858 464346   Fax 0858 434734.

British and International Golf Greenkeepers Association

BIGGA, as a professional organisation, was formed as recently as 1987, being an amalgamation of three smaller volunteer-led national associations. It now has over 5,000 members, organised into five regions and twenty five sections.

Its main objects and activities are :

* To promote and advance all aspects of greenkeeping
* To run the BTME (see below) and National Education and other conferences and courses for members
* To publish *Greenkeeping International*, a monthly magazine sent to all its members
* To promote the education and training of greenkeepers and to maintain a close relationship with the Greenkeepers Training Committee (see below) and other golfing bodies.

BIGGA awards Master Greenkeeper Certificates annually to Course Managers and Head Greenkeepers who have completed the required programme of theoretical and practical work.

The BTME (BIGGA Turf Management Exhibition) in six years has become the leading exhibition for suppliers of machinery and materials connected with all aspects of golf course maintenance. It is held in Harrogate in January of each year.   Workshops and seminars are held alongside the exhibition. Although the week is primarily for the benefit and education of greenkeepers, both Golf Club Secretaries and Green Chairmen would find much of interest touring the exhibition or attending the workshops or seminars.

Executive Director : Neil Thomas. Aldwark Manor, Aldwark, Alne, York YO6 2NF. Tel. 0347 838581/2 Fax 0347 838864.

The Golf Foundation

Founded in 1952, The Golf Foundation exists to promote the development of junior golf throughout the UK, especially for children who parents are not themselves golfers. Famous golfers such as Brian Barnes and Ronan Rafferty are amongst the thousands who have benefited from instruction under the its coaching scheme for Schools and Junior Groups. Its other activities include awarding promising youngsters vouchers for individual tuition, operating a Merit Award Scheme with set targets to measure progress, arranging open coaching centres in school holidays, arranging schools and age group championships, etc.

The Golf Foundation is dependent on donations to fund its work, and is grateful to the many golfers, Clubs and other organisations who continue to support it.

Executive Director: Miss Lesley Attwood MBE. Foundation House, Hanbury Manor, Ware, Herts. SG12 0UH. Tel 0920 484044 Fax 0920 484055.

The Greenkeepers Training Committee

This organisation is based alongside BIGGA with whom it maintains a close link. Funded by the R & A, the Home Unions and the PGA European Tour, it has now become responsible through its Education Unit, for the education and training of greenkeepers throughout the UK. Its activities include producing an excellent loose-leaf *Greenkeepers' Training Manual*, training videos (with BIGGA) , assessing and improving colleges at which greenkeepers may receive training, and arranging training programmes for greenkeepers at all levels. On the latter, the GTC will on request, and at no cost, provide a Club with a recommended training programme for each member of its green staff.

The GTC has carried out a Health & Safety survey amongst Golf Clubs. David Golding, its enthusiastic Education Director, has also been helping the Health and Safety Executive produce its *Guidance Notes for Golf Course Management*, published in June 1994.

Education Director : David Golding. Aldwark Manor, Aldwark, Alne, York, Y06 2NF. Tel. 0347 838640 Fax 0347 838775.

The Joint Golf Course Committee

The JGCC was formed in 1991 to try to ensure that the objectives set out in the R & A's booklet *The Way Forward* were fulfilled. The Committee's members are representatives from the R & A and Home Unions.

Its term of reference were :

*   To recommend standards of golf course construction and maintenance
*   To work with the Home Unions and others for the improvement of educational and professional standards in greenkeeping
*   To promote golf related research
*   To ensure availability of effective agronomic and technical advice
*   To encourage more effective Committee structures and the formation of long term management plans within Clubs
*   To raise funds in furtherance of these stated objectives.

Since then it has been successful in establishing the GTC Training Committee's Education Unit (see above) and ensuring its proper funding. It has also been instrumental in the setting up of the European Golf Association Ecology Unit, and again organising its proper financing. It is working closely with the STRI on items of research and is involved in discussions with the Committee of European Normalisation who are attempting to establish performance and construction standards for sports surfaces throughout Europe. Much of this work is being undertaken by its Technical Panel comprising representatives from the STRI, constructors, architects, greenkeepers, etc.

Executive Consultant: Eric Shiel.   Corner House, Blacksmith's Lane, Wellingore, Lincs, LN5 0HP.   Tel. 0522 811060 Fax 0522 810706.

The National Golf Clubs' Advisory Association

Founded in 1922, the NGCAA's purpose is in general to protect the interest of Golf Clubs, and in particular to give legal advice and direction (often backed by Counsels' opinion) whenever it is consulted by one of its member Clubs.

John Crowther, the Secretary of the NGCAA, has had many years relevant experience, both as Secretary of a Golf Club and as Secretary of the AGCS. His book *Managing Your Golf Club* makes interesting and helpful reading and may be ordered from him at the NGCAA, price £18.50 inc. p. & p. He also runs a three day residential course for those wishing to become Golf Club Secretaries.

Secretary : John Crowther. Angel House, Portland Square, Bakewell, Derbyshire DE45 1HB. Tel. 0629 813844 Fax 0629 812614.

The Professional Golfers' Association

The PGA was founded in 1901 and is now divided into seven regions. Its main aims are

* To promote interest in golf
* To protect and advance its members' interests
* To hold tournaments for its members
* To help members find employment, and in other appropriate ways.

It also has responsibility for arranging and obtaining sponsorship for the Ryder Cup and for running various PGA and other championships primarily for its members.

Anyone wishing to become a Club professional (and therefore a member of the PGA) has to undergo a minimum of three years training and to qualify at the PGA Training School. The first six months of that training is a probationary period during which the trainee retains his or her amateur status.

Executive Director: Sandy Jones. PGA National Headquarters, Apollo House, The Belfry, Sutton Coldfield, West Midlands B76 9PT Tel. 0675 470333 Fax 0675 470674.

The PGA European Tour

Membership is only open to professionals possessing certain minimum standards determined by its tournament Committee. A gruelling Qualifying School is held each year at which the top 40 leading players are awarded cards allowing them to play in PGA European Tour events the following season.

The Monday pre-qualifying tournament for each PGA European Tournament was abolished in 1985, when entries became all exempt.

The PGA European Tour in also involved with the organisation of the Ryder Cup, as a joint venture with the PGA.

Executive Director : Kenneth D Schofield. PGA European Tour, Wentworth Drive, Virginia Water, Surrey GU25 4LX.   Tel. 0344 842881 Fax 0344 842929.

The Sports Turf Research Institute

The STRI's principal objectives are to carry out research, and to provide advice and education, on all aspects of sports turf. It does this in three ways :

(1) Research

STRI began as the Board of Greenkeeping Research, and over the years has carried out many projects concerning the best methods of construction of golf greens, tees, bunkers, etc. and the most effective drainage systems. Its work on the most suitable varieties of grass for different purposes, the results of which are published annually in its *Turfgrass Seed* booklet, is recognised as an established authority on the subject. Other research studies have included nutrition and irrigation, wearability, and turfgrass pests and diseases.

(2) Advisory Service, comprising

- The care and maintenance of established courses
- Design and construction work, from the addition or re-siting of one green to a complete 18 hole course
- Ecological studies, to meet the needs of an increasing environmentally-conscious world, including advice on course on Sites of Special Scientific Interest (SSSIs) on or adjoining the course, and on the management of woodlands.

(3) Education, through

- Courses at their own premises for greenkeepers (and groundsmen), with condensed versions for Secretaries and Green Chairmen
- Seminars throughout the country
- A range of publications.

The STRI is a wholly independent, non-profit making organisation with the constitution of a Company limited by guarantee. The guarantors include the R & A, the four Home Unions, the AGCS, the PGA European Tour, CONGU, BIGGA and BAGCA. It also has the support of governing bodies from many other sports.

Its publications include an annual journal containing technical research articles and a quarterly *Sports Turf Bulletin* which has shorter and simpler contributions from its staff on a variety of subjects, the majority of which concern the upkeep of golf courses. These and other STRI books can be obtained direct from them.

Director: Peter Hayes. Secretary : T R Wheeldon. Bingley, West Yorkshire BD16 1AU. Tel. 0274 565131 Fax 0274 561891.

Other Associations of possible interest

Artisans Golfers' Association
Hon Sec: A Everett. 51 Rose Hill Park West, Sutton, Surrey SM1 3LA. Tel. 081 644 7037.

Golf Club Stewards' Association
Secretary: G Shaw. 50 The Park, St Albans, Herts. Tel 0727 857334.

Golf Society of Great Britain
Members enjoy discounted green fees on many well-known courses and can also participate in GSGB tournaments.
Secretary: Mrs EJ Drummond. Southview, Thurlestone, Devon TQ7 3NT. Tel 0548 560630.

Hole in One Golf Society
Secretary : B Dickenson. PO Box 109, New Lane, Greengates, Bradford, Yorkshire BD10 9UY Tel: 0274 618931.

Institute of Groundsmanship
Offers advisory services on all turf-related matters, staffing etc. It also runs educational courses throughout the country, and **SALTEX** (the Sports Amenities Landscaping Trade Exhibition) at the Royal Windsor racecourse annually each September.

Company Secretary : John Macfarlane. 19-23 Church Street, The Agora, Wolverton, Milton Keynes, Bucks. MK12 5LG. Tel. 0908 312511 Fax 0908 311140.

National Association of Public Golf Courses
Hon. Sec. : A K Witte. 35 Sinclair Grove, Golders Green, London NW11 9JH. Tel. 081 458 5433.

Society of One-Armed Golfers
Hon. Sec. : Don Reid. 11 Coldwell Lane, Filling, Tyne & Wear, NE10 9EX. Tel. 091 469 4742.

Public Schools' Old Boys' Golf Association
Responsible for organising the annual Grafton Morrish tournament.
Joint Secretary: P A de Pinna, Bruins, Wythwood, Haywards Heath, West Sussex RH16 4RD Tel. 0444 454833 (home) 071 265 0071 (office).

Public Schools' Golfing Society

Responsible for organising the annual Halford Hewitt tournament.
Hon. Sec. : J N S Lowe, Flushing House, Church Road, Great Bookham, Surrey KT23 3JT.   Tel. 0372 458 651.

18
Golf Competitions and Miscellaneous

This Chapter contains a few ideas and suggestions which, if new to your Club, may prove to be enjoyable events for your members, or helpful in the running of the Club.

Golf Competitions

A **5 Club knockout** competition during the winter months, will attract a large entry.

A **Foursomes Reel** is a competition format which has proved to be popular amongst players in a 36 hole foursomes event, particularly when it is taking place on another course.

Play is as in normal foursomes except that players change partners within their team of four every six holes, so that by the end of the round each will have played six holes partnering each other. Different teams are arranged for the afternoon round to enable each competitor then to play six holes foursomes with three new partners.

The recommended allowance for medal or stableford scoring is 1/6th of the combined handicaps for each six hole segment. In stableford competitions, the strokes are taken at the lowest stroke index holes within the segment. Each player records his own score.

Prizes are given for individual and team scores. Additionally, a golf ball can be offered to both members of a pair scoring 13 or more stableford points over the six holes, as a way of maintaining interest for everyone throughout the day.

An **alternative foursomes** format is one under which each player chooses in advance at which 9 of the 18 holes he would like to drive. This can be decided in rotation i.e. the two players take turns to choose a hole until all 18 holes have been selected by each. A further rule can be introduced under which both players have to share the short holes between them.

A "**Yellow Ball**" is a vicious but enjoyable competition, ideal for 9 holes in the evening. Under this format, play is in teams of three, each person taking it in turn to play a hole with a yellow ball. The net score of the yellow ball plus the better of the other two players' scores count as the team score for each hole.

A **Texas Scramble** seems to be popular as an occasional event. There are various methods of handicapping but one which has proved to be fair for all combinations of players (in teams of four playing 18 holes) is on the following somewhat complex formula :

(a) Multiply each player's handicap as follows :
Lowest handicap x 4
Second lowest handicap x 3
Third lowest handicap x 2
Highest handicap x 1

(b) Divide the total of those figures by 10, and take 3/4 of the answer to give the team's stroke allowance.

Example:

Player A is 2 handicap, Player B is 10, Player C is 18 and Player D is 28.

Calculation:	A:	2 x 4 =	8
	B:	10 x 3 =	30
	C:	18 x 2 =	36
	D:	28 x 1 =	28
Total			102
Divide by 10			= 10.2

3/4 of 10.2 = 7.65 = 8 strokes deducted from medal score.

Invitation Mixed Foursomes played over 18 holes starting at around 1.30 pm, followed by dinner in the clubhouse and prize-giving, is a welcome alternative to the more usual arrangement of providing a large lunch with 18 or 36 holes being played during the day.

In the **Druce Trophy** played by Surrey Ladies, a pair from each competing Club plays 18 holes foursomes in the morning, recording their net medal score at each hole. The Club's second pair then play 18 holes foursomes in the afternoon, and have to try to improve on the team's morning score at each hole. Each of the two pairs must consist of a member of the Silver and Bronze handicap divisions.

Variable handicap allowance is a form of competition suitable for days like Boxing Day or New Year's Day. It is a single or foursomes event which each player adds strokes to his handicap depending upon on the number of clubs he carries for the round. The scale of allowances might be - assuming one club must be a putter :

For 8 or more clubs	Nil
7 clubs	1
6 "	2
5 "	4
4 "	7
3 "	10
2 "	13

Captain's Day formats obviously vary greatly from Club to Club. One very popular and friendly competition is simply a three ball, better ball, medal team event, each team consisting of a low, medium and a high handicap golfer. The lowest net score by any one of the three players counts as the team score at each hole.

Playing the course backwards or over a special cross country course is another event many Clubs hold once a year in the evening. One Club combines this with an annual long driving competition.

A **Dawn Patrol** competition involving a shotgun start at say 5 am followed by "Bucks Fizz" and breakfast is usually well supported.

Challenge Matches between categories of members are also popular events. Teams might be President's v Captain's, Present v Past Committee, Young v Old, Accountants v Lawyers, or England v Scotland on the morning of the Calcutta match.

Miscellaneous Items

150 yard markers

These distance markers to centres of greens are appearing on more and more courses, and are particularly appreciated by visitors. Hopefully too, they speed up play as they lessen the need for the yardage charts to be deciphered. Discreet posts nor more than 2 feet high placed on the edge of the rough by each fairway are more visible than white spots or concrete markers in the centre of fairways.

Slow play is a continuing problem for which the only cures seem to be having a Course Marshal or a vigilant Secretary out on the course at peak times, frequent warnings to regular offenders, and reminders on places like the scorecard.

Too many notices on the course can become an irritant.

Water savings in the clubhouse can be achieved if the men's locker room is fitted with a gadget which, though an infra red beam, ensures that the urinals are only flushed after they have been used, instead of regularly every few minutes.

Bridge, both amongst members and in matches against other Clubs, is becoming more and more popular. Provided it does not detract from the Club being primarily a Golf Club for golfers, bridge can be a useful source of additional revenue for the bar and dining room.

Tee reservations for Societies or for Club events are usually recorded on a notice board situated in a highly visible spot. Some Clubs now arrange to produce copies of a typed version, at fortnightly intervals, for members to take away.

Photographs of honour boards and of the Club's trophies are a useful safeguard against fire or theft.

Appendix 1
A Thankless Task

Jim Arthur offers some advice as to how new recruits to the Green Committee can best equip themselves to make an effective contribution.

I am somewhat handicapped in offering any advice because for forty-five years I have maintained that we do not need Green Committees but instead a defined management structure - in other words a written policy document, implemented by an amiable dictator.   One is reminded of Howard Keel's response on being invited to chair the Green Committee of his own Club (on the grounds that anyone who could control J R Ewing in Dallas would find a Golf Club easy work).   He made two conditions, first that the membership should be an uneven number, and second that three was too many.

However, this is a far from perfect world.   Management policies, though advocated for decades have never been universally adopted or even accepted (often due to lack of guidance or to a reluctance to change) and dictators sometimes do not stay amiable!

Assuming that Bill Smith, who is known to be keen as well as critical, is therefore invited to join the Green Committee, even if only to control and direct his enthusiasm, what should he do?   The first and most obvious recipe for success is to stay silent and listen for a reasonable period and I do not mean just the first meeting.   Secondly education is never wasted. The problem is usually the source and quality of that education.

A sensible recruit wishing to learn will go to the man who knows his course better than anyone else - the Head Greenkeeper.   When I first started advisory work just after the war, I was trained by a brilliant botanist, the senior adviser at Bingley.   He told me something I have never forgotten.   "Listen to what the head man has to say most attentively - if he isn't talking find out why".   Go and make a real friend of your Head Greenkeeper and see how you can help him.

Long suffering head men faced with constantly changing Committees and as many changes of policy, have found that the best answer is token agreement, masterly inactivity and silent pursuit of their own consistent policy.   If that is the right policy, success is assured!

I remember from the days when I was the agronomist to the R & A's Championship Committee, I was given the daunting task of getting Turnberry ready (from a state of near, if not total, disaster) for their first Open - with less than three seasons in which to reverse all the wrong previous policies.   In pursuance of this change I had the wholehearted support of both the Hotel (then British Transport Hotels) and the head greenkeeper Jim McCubbin.   Jim, however, somewhat naturally lacked experience in presenting an Open Championship - so we invited the head man from another Championship course for a week to guide him on these matters.   They started talking about the differences in managerial control and direction between a hotel and a private Club.   Jim, who said he was responsible only to one man - the hotel manager (Chris Rouse, still doing a remarkable job on hotel and courses), and opined that working for a Committee especially when the Chairman changed every year must be hell.   "On the contrary", was the reply, "When the new man comes in, I assure him that for the next three months I have to complete his predecessor's programme and then I will start on his.   The next three months are difficult - with the Chairman realising that he is not going to get his own way.   During the third three months, as soon as I see him coming on the course, I leave by another route and I take my holidays in that period".   "What about the fourth three months?   It must be impossible!"   "On the contrary, no problem - he has given up by then"!

By all means read background literature and articles and attend seminars, but only to help your understanding.   Do not think that in a short period you can equip yourself to advise anyone with vastly greater practical experience and knowledge.   Forget all about your own cherished theories. Debate them, if you must, with head men, or visiting advisers, but be prepared to have them dismissed.   Remember the old adage, "Ask a farmer what to do and go and do exactly the opposite".   Remember, too, that the Head Greenkeeper's pet hate is the man with a super lawn.   How much traffic does that lawn get - how sheltered is it in contrast to often very exposed golf greens?   In any case nice and green lawns may please householders, but "nice and green" is anathema to good greenkeepers.

Serving successfully on a Green Committee hinges on acceptance of the terms and conditions of the function of that Committee.   It is easier to stress what it is not. Its function most emphatically is not to give orders to an experienced head man on how to run his course. Incidentally, it is a Green Committee, never "Greens". It covers the whole of the course - not just the greens.

Perhaps the best way to emphasise its proper function is to compare it with running a company - the difference between direction and management. When the Chairman of the Board starts telling the Works Manager how to run the factory, Carey Street looms close ahead!

Of course, faults are never one-sided. There are still inexperienced, weak, misguided, idle, obstinate and wrong-headed Head Greenkeepers pointed firmly in the wrong direction. If they want something quite opposite to the desires of the Club - even if the Club may be equally wrong-headed - the only answer, apart from unlikely death-bed conversions, is for the Head Greenkeeper to look for a fresh post, but be sure that either he resigns or the correct disciplinary procedures are followed before he is given notice by the Club. Recent cases of wrongful dismissal, virtually always favouring the head man, have proved costly.

Education, now with so much better facilities and funding, will resolve some of the problems of bad earlier training or lack of it. If a new entrant Green Committee member also wishes to take advantage of such facilities, it must be solely with the object of understanding problems and appreciating difficulties and never to set himself up as a surrogate Head Greenkeeper.

To sum up, in my view the proper functions of the Green Committee are:

- To fight for a fair share (or better) of available funds to be spent on the course and not the clubhouse

- To listen to and sieve the views of members and to explain why meeting the often selfish demands of minorities can disrupt the future enjoyment of the course by the majority

- To lay down agreed policies and broad direction, and

- To co-opt the Head Greenkeeper as the practical expert in implementing it. Keeping dogs and barking oneself has never been a good way of running things.

Teamwork is the secret of success - and this means at times that Head Greenkeepers must see problems from the Club's viewpoint and accept modest levels of damage in pursuit of keeping members on full greens as long as possible - with less of the attitude expressed to me by one old Scots greenkeeper - who really meant it - that if only he could get rid of yon dratted golfers he could always have **his** course in perfect order !

Good luck to you, you glutton for punishment. Accept that you will get no thanks but will be the recipient of all the grumbles - most of which will be outside your control !

Appendix 2
R & A Publications

Books and Leaflets

Decisions on the Rules of Amateur Status	£6 in Europe
	£8 elsewhere
Decisions on the Rules of Golf (1994 Edition)	£16.00 (GB & I)
	£19.00 (Europe)
	£21.00 (Elsewhere)
Golf Rules Illustrated*	£7.99 (Exc. P&P)
Golf Rules in Brief (card)	Free of charge
Guidance for Club Committees on the Making of Local Rules and Other Matters	Free of charge
Duties of Referees and Committee Members	Free of charge
Recommendations regarding hole positions	Free of charge
Guidelines for team matches	Free of charge
Guideline for suspension of play	Free of charge
The Way Forward (1988)	£2.50
The Demand for Golf (November 1989)	£4.50

Videos

First Nine Holes Rule Course (featuring John Glover - Rules Secretary R&A)	£10.99 (+ P&P)
Second Nine Holes Rule Course (featuring John Glover)	£10.99 (+ P&P)
BBC Video Golf: A Royal & Ancient Game (featuring Steve Rider, Helen Wadsworth and John Glover)	£10.99 (+ P&P)
On Course Rules Instruction (featuring John Glover)	£10.99 (+ P&P)

* *This title available from Reed Book Services Tel. 0933 410511.*

The other publications and videos may be ordered from the Royal & Ancient Golf Club of St Andrews, Fife, KY16 9JD Tel. 0334 472112 Fax 0334 477580.

Index